How to Make

BIG
MONEY
GROOMING
SMALL DOGS

The absolute amateur's guide

to profitable, professional

canine styling

Robert S. Whitman
Author and illustrator

First Edition

Library of Congress Catalog Card Number: 93-87742

ISBN: paperback 0-9640215-1-X

ISBN: casebound 0-9640215-0-1

The author has tried to make the contents as accurate as possible. However, due to variability of local conditions, personal skill, etc., neither the author nor publisher assumes responsibility for injury, damage, or other losses incurred that may result from the use or misuse of the material presented herein. All instructions should be carefully studied and clearly understood before beginning work with any animal.

THIS PUBLICATION IS DESIGNED TO PROVIDE ACCURATE AND AUTHORITATIVE INFORMATION IN REGARD TO THE SUBJECT MATTER COVERED. IT IS SOLD WITH THE UNDERSTANDING THAT THE PUBLISHER IS NOT ENGAGED IN RENDERING LEGAL, ACCOUNTING OR OTHER PROFESSIONAL SERVICE. IF LEGAL ADVICE OR OTHER EXPERT ASSISTANCE IS REQUIRED, THE SERVICES OF A COMPETENT PROFESSIONAL PERSON SHOULD BE SOUGHT.

(From a Declaration of Principles jointly adopted by a Committee of the American Bar Association and a Committee of Publishers.)

Printed in the United States of America
First printing 1995
Second printing 2001

Published by:
Protective Specialties Development Group
P.O. Box 39060
Philadelphia PA 19136

DEDICATION

To my family

My wife, Eileen, and my two sons, Scott and Drew, without whose help and encouragement this work would never have been completed.

And to my past clients

All the Jyminees, Bitsys, Krimpets, and Fifis. Their patient small bodies made it possible to formulate, develop, and prove the humane methods described and pictured within these pages.

Acknowledgment

Many thanks to my editor, Richard Carson, for his patience and skill in refining my writings into an organized text.

Foreword

Each year thousands of canine pets of various breeds must have their coats shaved off — sacrificed — due to their owners' lack of knowledge or ability to properly brush and comb in order to maintain them. Improper maintenance leads to snarled, tangled, felted coats. In the grooming industry, this is referred to as matting.

This information is designed to overcome the problem of matted coats through step-by-step instruction in the proper handling of the animal and equipment alike. Do not be confused by what is usually found in the average dog care books. Contained herein are the same unique, highly detailed methods used successfully for more than 25 years in Pennsylvania's first professionally licensed trade school for canine styling and grooming.

The application of these methods, formerly available only to registered students, will enable you to become skilled in the required procedures. When applied to your own dog, these methods will prevent matting and animal discomfort. You will save the charge usually incurred in grooming matted canines, and preserve your pet's good looks and health as well.

Never before has a work such as this been written, for it takes nothing for granted. The fears of approach by a new student, and potential harm of animal or student, have been accounted for and handled in a most exacting way to avoid either.

The precise detail of the text and illustrations is unique for a work of this type.

The author spent many months reviewing and revising drafts of the text and his portfolio of sketches. The goal? To produce instructions and illustrations so accurate, that when processed into graphics, would clearly translate his precise directions. With this precision and clarity achieved, the student-reader could easily understand and practice the lessons given. The end result is a book that delivers dog grooming and styling instructions previously unavailable at any price.

The instruction has been written by Robert S. Whitman, founder and director of the Pennsylvania School of Dog Grooming, in Philadelphia, Pennsylvania, a state-licensed facility founded in 1969.

Incorporated in the text are all the special methods that have been taught at Pennsylvania School of Dog Grooming, for safe, fast, accurate grooming without the sacrifice of animal welfare.

Here, then, is a convenient way to learn canine styling on your own, from an authority on the subject. In the comfort of your own home, you may learn to master new and enlightening procedures to perfection, while acquiring a skill any animal owner would be proud to command. It's the next best thing to in-person instruction. If you now own a Poodle or similar breed, or can beg for, borrow, or buy one, then your first requirement will have been completed.

Table of Contents

List of Illustrations

About This Book

When you open and thumb through the first few sections of this guidebook, do not be surprised by the apparent lack of fancy show dog photos, on slick high gloss papers.

You see, this book is intended to teach, guide, and motivate you to achieve success in pet grooming using the specific methods outlined.

It is the books *information* that is designed to satisfy your desire for knowledge in this field; and not the glitz or glamour of it's contents.

Glamour eventually fades, but *information* leads to knowledge.

Robert S. Whitman

Tools Of The Trade ✔✔

New aspiring painters will usually purchase a wide variety of brushes, canvas and other paraphernalia. Eventually, they settle for a *few*, which they find are all that are needed. So it is with "Canine Artists"!

The tools illustrated here are of the same type as those discussed throughout the various chapters of this book. Although the exact same models are not required to do a decent grooming job, these however are th*e type of tools* that are recommended.

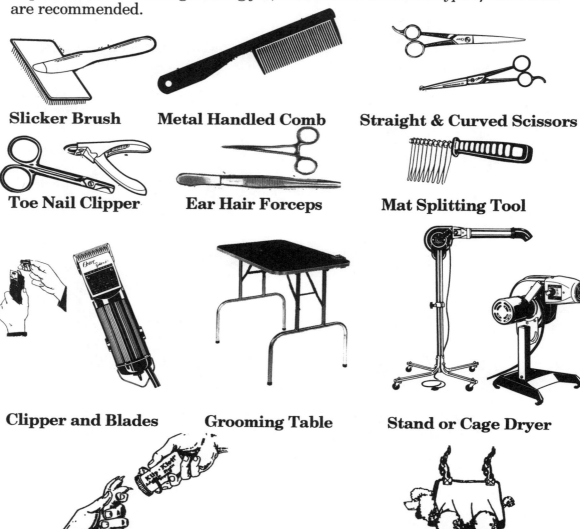

Slicker Brush **Metal Handled Comb** **Straight & Curved Scissors**

Toe Nail Clipper **Ear Hair Forceps** **Mat Splitting Tool**

Clipper and Blades **Grooming Table** **Stand or Cage Dryer**

Klip-Klot ® Automatic Styptic **Clippin' Sling ® System Set**

Optional tools would include: caging of various types, CaddyPillar ® ribbon bow dispenser, Electric nail groomer, thinning shears, Control Leashes and Choker Chain, Bath Spray Control., portable Clippin' Sling table support bracket, and of course a dedicated Bathing Station. Remember ...add tools slowly, and only those that are needed!

The importance of grooming

How much is that doggie in the window? How much did your doggie cost? Just how much is he or she worth to you? If you are like most pet owners, your answer will probably be, "Why he or she's priceless, a member of our family, and you can't place a dollar value on family, can you?"

That is just the point: You can't place a high enough value on all the love, fun and affection a pet can return to you simply for the expense of a minimum amount of proper care. The attitude of some who say, "I feed him, walk him, and let the groomer do the rest," should not be the position of one who truly values the health and well-being of the loyal family pet.

In order to maintain those things that first caused you to purchase that cuddly bundle of fur, a few other steps are required on a regular basis. The key word is "regular."

To better understand the principles of animal health through proper care and grooming, we first must analyze what it is that gives our groomable pets those characteristics they possess.

The most obvious thing noted when you purchased your "fuzzy" puppy was the furry coat the animal came wrapped in. The same thing that makes them so cuddly can be the thing that can turn you off to your pet, if not properly maintained.

All dogs shed! Now that may sound contrary to what you were told when you purchased your glamour breed, but it is a fact of nature that when the light of day lengthens or shortens, as it does when the season changes, your dog will shed its previous season's coat, just as humans do. The problem, however, is that where we simply hang up our season's discard, a dog's coat must be physically removed in order to keep him or her in a condition we can enjoy in a house pet.

Now let's get right to it. An ungroomed dog, one that does not get regular brushing, combing, bathing, and in the case of glamour breeds (Poodles, etc.), clipping after a while will be a total mess — unattractive, foul-smelling, dirty and in some cases obviously frightening-looking.

Hair and fur will overgrow the anus, making it near impossible to defecate without a residue remaining on the coat. This will build in size with each bowel movement until it gets to such an extent that you won't want to be in the dog's presence, and it will be a cause of irritation to the animal as it would if it were human.

Overgrowth in the genital area can cause urine scald irritation, similar to diaper rash. Naturally, fur that is urine-saturated has a very ugly offensive odor as well. As urine dries with each urination, it can crystalize on the genitals, increasing the degree of irritation and irritability of the animal. All of this is basically because the animal requires care in these areas.

To further complicate the situation, the shedding will cause matting of the coat if not properly handled. During the life of the animals we see in school, 50% are brought in at least once in such a condition that the pet must be clipped extremely close to the skin to remove a coat that, due to neglect or improper care, has matted. Matting comes about as a result of loose shedded fur being allowed to remain in certain or all areas of the animal's body.

As the dog moves, lies down, scratches or bites at itself, combined with a possible wetting of the coat due to rain, drinking splash, or owner's bathing, the loose fur compresses to form a felt layer close to the skin line. This felted coat cannot be pulled out with a comb, lest you tear the skin or, at the very least, pull out the live hair or fur along with the dead. As the fur mats further it draws the skin tight in areas that normally tend to stretch with the pet's motion, and causes discomfort. The uncomfortable situation may cause the animal to bite at itself, trying to gain relief, and even to pull out large patches of fur, leaving bare places in the coat. When in this condition, the skin is open to secondary conditions such as fungus, bacterial and insect-caused infections. It is near impossible to treat a dog for fleas, mites, lice or ticks when heavily matted, and these parasites can cause internal as well as external health problems.

Most common is the problem caused by fleas. Those dogs who are allergic to the flea's bite will scratch due to an allergic reaction to the flea's digestive juices, which are poured into the wound that is produced. The dog then develops a rash, which itches fiercely. The itching sensation causes the dog to scratch and bite at the area in order to gain some relief and often swallow a flea at the same time. Since the flea is the host carrier for the tapeworm parasite, the dog now becomes the new home for the worm's next generation with all of its added health problems.

Proper grooming is not a job for a small child. Many a time I have seen adults blame the poor condition of their pet on their children's lack of care, because they bought it for them.

It requires an adult to properly brush and comb a pup or full-grown pet to the point that the animal accepts it as a biweekly routine at minimum, without resistance. As the animal becomes used to the grooming, adults may teach a child whose age and strength are such that it is capable of the job to care for the pet, while being supervised.

Only regular proper care will produce the results you originally fell in love with when you first saw that furry doggie in the window.

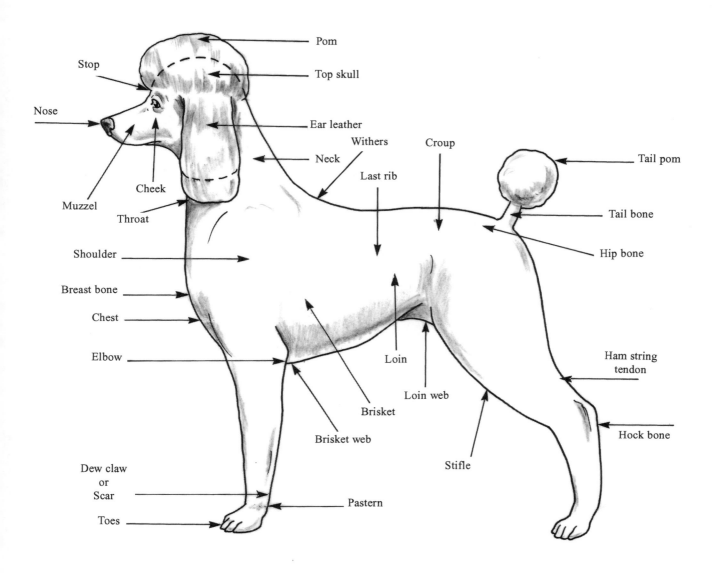

Canine Anatomy

PROPER BRUSHING METHOD
Using a Slicker Brush

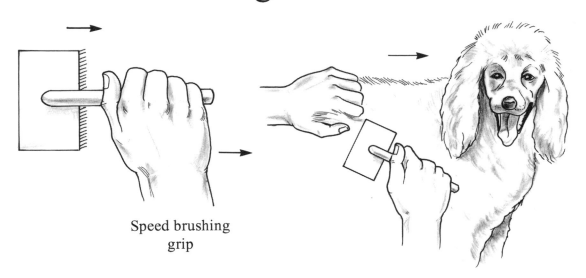

Speed brushing
grip

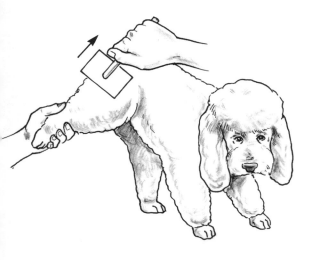

Brushing
AGAINST
the grain

Brushing
WITH
the grain

Head - Tail - Ears
ONLY

Brushing and combing

I am now going to instruct you in the same method of brushing and combing taught at PSDG that has been used successfully on thousands of animals. It is safe, fast, efficient, and produces the satisfactory results necessary to keep your pet healthy and looking good.

Purchase a brush with a T-shaped handle known as a slicker. These have the grasping handle at right angles to the wire brush pad, which is composed of short, closely spaced curved wire bristles. The shape and closeness of the wire bristles are what is needed to extract the dead and dying fur from the dog's coat. Soft human hair brushes and straight pin brushes won't do the job. Next get an all metal-handled, medium-spaced comb. This will be used after the brushing to check the quality of the brushing procedure. A metal comb will not create static as will a hard rubber or plastic comb, such as is used for human hair. Static is one of the causes of hair snarls. A handled comb will make holding it much more controllable for you and more comfortable for the dog as well, since if the proper angle is not maintained the animal's skin may be scraped in sensitive areas.

A table of suitable working height must be used. Anything that is solid, not shaky, will do. Provide a non-slip surface such as a rubber or carpet mat for the top of the table, so that the dog will not slide and can feel surefooted and safe. If not, he/she will want to jump off to get to solid ground; however, the floor is where he plays, walks, and runs, and it is not the place to attempt to groom.

When trained to a table, the pet associates it with the grooming process and will cooperate in a way he never would on the floor.

He must be trained to know that the floor is there for freedom, and the table for business: brushing, combing, clipping, etc.

Not essential, but recommended, is a grooming spray. These are formulated to provide a light lubricant to the coat so that brushing won't break already brittle split ends on dry coats. The use of the spray lets the brush and comb slip through the coat easier, with less trauma.

Now you are ready to help your pet to a healthier coat and skin, and a better life.

Start by placing your pet on the table and command the dog to "stay." Don't play with it now, but demand obedience. You want your pet to be still in a standing position looking away from you, while you stand behind its rear. Now, grasp the neck coat with your left hand and draw it tight towards you.

Pick up the slicker brush in your right hand and turn your hand until the handle in your grasp is pointing towards the dog's head. You will now start to brush by pushing the brush in light contact with the coat ahead of that in your left hand. Your right hand moves up with the brush as your left hand pulls the coat down, both hands moving opposite each other. Starting at the neck, stroke the coat a series of times working from side to side until the brush moves through it smoothly as dead fur accumulates in the brush. Use the comb to remove it. Don't rush it. Don't force it. Use more action and less pressure to do the job without hurting the animal.

Always remember that there is flesh under the fur. Even though you may not see it, it still can be injured. When the brush has penetrated the coat and is moving easily and smoothly, take a new grasp on the area below it with the left hand and continue to brush from side to side until the whole back and side portion is finished, down to the tail. All the time keep in your position, and make sure your dog remains standing so that you are to the rear of it. This enables you to brush against the lay of the coat. The coat grows from head to tail. Tail to head we will call *against the grain.*

When the back brushing is finished, still standing at the rear, grasp the right front leg, lift it forward and brush the coat on the dog's right front chest area *against the grain.* Next do the same on the left, by lifting the left front leg up and out in front. When brushing *against the grain,* lifting the legs tightens the skin in those areas to facilitate proper brushing.

Next, place your left hand between the dog's hind legs, hold your hand in a handshake position, and grasp the right hind leg high up in the groin area. Use your index finger to depress and tighten the skin at the point where the leg joins the abdomen.

Now control the dog and command "stay" if it should move around while you are working. Brush the right side of the abdomen *against the grain.* Repeat on the left side, taking an outside-the-leg grip by using your left hand in a handshake position, grasping the left leg high on the outside thigh from behind so as to enable you to wrap your index finger around and press into the groin area. This pressure protects the web of skin that joins the leg to the abdomen from abrasion from the brush. You must cross over from the right to the left side, with your right hand still holding the brush, and brush *against the grain.*

Using the same hand grasps as when doing the abdomen, brush the hind legs, starting at the hip and working down to the foot, stroking *against the grain.* Do the outside, front edge and back edge of each leg. Then lift one leg, allowing it to bend so you have access to the inside of the opposite leg, and brush the inside lightly. Repeat the same process on the opposite hind leg. As you raise each leg, be sure to help the dog retain balance by not lifting the foot higher than the spine. Be sure not to hold the leg too low either. Adjust the height until the dog is well balanced on its three legs with you giving support to the fourth.

Grasp the tail in your left hand with your thumb pointing to the ceiling. Hold the tail close to the spine as you would hold a flag. Carefully brush *against the grain* the coat on either side of the anus, but don't go over the anus itself. Work very carefully, as this is a very sensitive area and prone to injury.

Brushing and combing sequence

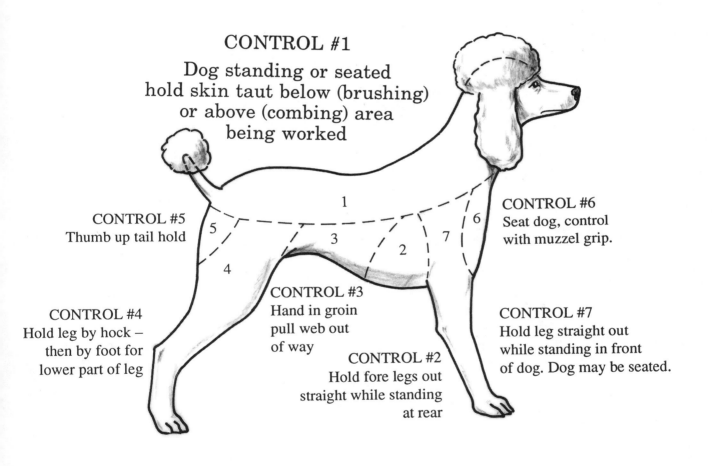

CONTROL #1
Dog standing or seated
hold skin taut below (brushing)
or above (combing) area
being worked

CONTROL #5
Thumb up tail hold

CONTROL #6
Seat dog, control
with muzzel grip.

CONTROL #4
Hold leg by hock —
then by foot for
lower part of leg

CONTROL #3
Hand in groin
pull web out
of way

CONTROL #7
Hold leg straight out
while standing in front
of dog. Dog may be seated.

CONTROL #2
Hold fore legs out
straight while standing
at rear

The back legs now completed, turn the dog around to face you and command "sit" and physically cause the dog to sit still facing you. Remember that when you are at the head end you still should remain serious and not give the dog a reason to "break stay" and start to play. You may praise him and give him a pat on the head, but stick to business.

With the dog seated, place your thumb under the dog's chin and wrap your hand around the muzzle, mouth shut, to maintain a grip on the dog and lift the head to no more than a 45-degree angle. If lifted too high, the dog will not cooperate due to the uncomfortable position. Try tilting your own head way back and in that position try to swallow. You will better appreciate the dog's position, and perhaps better respect the reason for the 45-degree angle.

Now brush *against the grain* on the throat, chest, and between the front legs. Use care over the breastbone and light pressure on the throat. Provided that you brushed all areas without skipping over sections too quickly, you have now completed the dog's body.

Grasp his front left foot and brush *against the grain* all areas from shoulder to foot. When finished, grasp his right foot in your left hand, cross over with your right hand, and brush all areas *against the grain*. Don't forget the front and rear edges of the legs where the coat is usually fuller, and is more prone to mat on both the front and hind legs.

Hold one ear in your left hand, with the hand under the ear. With the ear leather laying in your palm, and the brush now held with the handle pointing towards yourself, brush *with the grain* by pulling the brush from the ear base toward the tip end. Be gentle; use light pressure and more action. Ears usually snag easily and you will probably have to do more work for the small area you are handling on the ears than you did on a equally sized area of the body.

Care must be exercised not to injure the delicate ear tissue, called the leather. Do not try to force the bristles through to the other side of the hair or the tassel or long ends of the ear hairs. Work steady at an even pressure, staying *with the grain*. Occasionally flip the ear over to the other side and stroke *with the grain*, also on the inside surface, until both surfaces are free of snags and dead hair.

Your brush is likely to load up with dead hair at this point, so use your comb through it to remove it. Don't continue to brush when the brush is loaded; it will not perform as it should unless it is free of accumulated dead hair.

When the ears are finished, brush the top of the head *with the grain*, using a similar muzzle grip used to do the throat: thumb over muzzle, hand wrapped around under chin. Now brush from front to back *with the grain*, but first command "stay."

The skin will be stretched tightly over the skull with no flesh under it to pad it. The skin can be easily abraded if too much pressure is exerted on the brush. Be sure to be thorough by starting your stroke just back of the eyes and finishing at the neck. Slow definite strokes rather than fast choppy ones are desired, and are less likely to cause discomfort.

Reverse the dog so that he is again facing away from you. Hold the tail with your palm under it and your thumb wrapped around on top. Since the bone in the tail has only skin and no fat or muscle over it, treat it gently and brush *with the grain* from base to tip. If the tail's tassel fringe or pompom is long, brush off the side of the bone to prevent abrasion.

Take the comb in your right hand, the tail in your left, and comb *with the grain.* Extreme care must he exercised not to scrape the skin and dig into it. Hold the comb at a 45-degree angle to the tail. If held at a lesser angle it is apt to pull and snag. At a greater angle it will rake over the hair but will not have the desired effect of removing snags and dead matted lumps and sections. If a snag is engaged and the comb can not go through, turn the comb so that the end is pointed toward the dog and only one tooth may be used to pick at and break up the tangle mat or snag. Then proceed with the regular 45-degree angle, combing *with the grain.* Use the same control positions as brushing to comb the rest of the dog. Starting with the back, however, now we will pull the comb with our right hand and hold back the coat with the left by holding and stretching the coat towards the head, both hands going in opposite directions.

When combing the chest and abdomen near the leg junctions, be cautious not to engage the webs of the skin that are attached at the areas equal to our own armpit and groin areas.

Combing *with the grain* at the rear under the tail must be restricted to below the anus and either side of it only. Do not comb directly over the anus. When combing *with the grain* over the legs, be sure not to engage the extra claws some dogs have on the legs just above the foot, causing them to have five nails. These "dewclaws" can be easily torn off the leg if care in combing this area is not used. Some dogs have them on the front legs, some on the back, some on all four legs, and some have two on each of the four legs!

The under-chest area may be combed if done with care not to comb too far back so as to engage the breasts on a female or penis on a male. It is also cautioned that physical contact be made with the hands first to determine the extent of projection on the under-area, such as tumors, larger nipples, etc. A common projection is an umbilical hernia. This is at the area of the navel and may be as small as a pea or as large as a walnut. A comb can easily tear the skin open if forced in this area. Absolutely no brushing or combing should be done in the area of the inner groin or genitals. The irritation that would result would be unbearable to the poor animal unfortunate enough to have these procedures performed in that area.

It is more desirable to comb the face *with the grain* rather than brush, since it is so delicate an area. Observe caution at the eyes, and at the areas on either side of the nose when combing use the muzzle grip. Work slowly and carefully at the mouth's corners.

Remember, these procedures have been tested and used on thousands of canines over the past 25 years without incident. They are fast, accurate, and above all safe when done as described. Don't deviate because you think it may be easier to do so until you have mastered a tested method.

At this point it is time to praise your pet for its cooperation. Genuinely show your appreciation; it is the best reward you can give.

Now sit back and admire the job you have done, and praise yourself for a job well done. It will benefit your pet with both good health and beauty.

Total time to complete it can be as little as 15 minutes.

Bathing, dipping, conditioning and hot oil treatments

Contrary to how it is depicted in most cartoons, most dogs do not object to the routine bath, provided that is not prepared or presented incorrectly.

The primary purpose of bathing is to make the animal clean. Simple statement, but it's surprising how many owners fail to see the purpose, and still believe that a bath is required only once a year.

Be aware that bacteria and microscopic parasites are always present on the animal's body, and a routine bath helps to accomplish more than what is visibly obvious. Besides making the animal look clean, it helps keep down the number of bacteria and parasites to the point of control. Left to multiply, these facts of nature can and do contribute to the ill health and misery some unfortunate animals suffer due to misinformation regarding their health habits.

Proper bathing can be a pleasant break in the overall grooming operation for both the groomer and the dog as well. It provides a change of pace, and a short rest for the dog from the required still position it must maintain when being brushed, combed and clipped to avoid injury.

The bath water at proper temperature is soothing to the skin and comforting, and gives the groomer the opportunity to relate to the animal on a more relaxed basis then is usually required for safety.

Start the bath by first having all required ingredients on hand. You don't want to start searching for the essentials once you have gotten the dog positioned in the tub, anticipating the bath. It's a good idea to secure the dog in the tub with a short leash or chain attached to a hook on the wall over the tub. This way, a wet soapy dog won't be a problem to contain in the bathtub should it decide that it doesn't want to be there. There are exceptions. If possible, preset the water temperature to just tepid, slightly more than lukewarm, so that you will neither chill nor burn the animal at first contact.

The dog may be stood in the tub on all four feet, or, if the bathing facility has an attached drain board section, the dog's front feet may rest on it. This in itself will offer more security to some animals, keeping their head elevated up higher from the tub floor and the water that accumulates in it.

It is advisable that the dog be shower bathed, rather than stood in a tub full of water. The benefit is reduced fear of being submersed, hence better cooperation during the bathing process. Shower bathing allows dirt and insects, live or dead, to be rinsed down the drain, and clean rinse water is constantly flushing the animal's coat as opposed to tub bathing, where the same dirt and insect-laden water is repeatedly thrown back over the animal in an attempt to completely flush all shampoo, etc., from the coat.

Dirty shampoo-laden rinse water can enter the eyes or mouth of the dog with possible ill effects, not to be realized until later, when the dog's illness wouldn't even be attributed to so simple a reason as the bath's being the vehicle.

In any case, a rubber ribbed mat should be placed in the tub to give a slip-proof place for the dog to stand on, the lack of which can cause the dog fear.

Various shampoos are available for every possible condition, use and taste. Basically they are either coat builders, color brighteners, softeners, or parasite killers, all designed to make the dog clean. While some may be tearless types, it is always advisable to protect the eyes from entrance of any type of shampoo, and to go the additional step of protecting them by dropping one drop of mineral oil, drugstore quality, in each eye prior to application of any type of parasite-killing solution, shampoo or dip.

Dip concentrates designed to kill parasites may be either chemical or botanical in formula, the later being desired due to its natural ingredients, which are less apt to cause allergic reactions or irritations on sensitive skins. Concentrates are diluted as specified by the manufacturer and then either sponged or poured over the body after bathing and rinsing.

The dip will not be rinsed off after application; it is most desirable to pour the dip so that any parasites such as fleas, lice, or mites will be flushed out as they are killed by the solution. This is hardly possible when sponging. Although some grooming facilities will salvage the used dip, strain and reuse it, I don't recommend this practice because the potency of the dip will change due to the dilution caused by the coat's being wet when dip is applied, to evaporation, and to the breakdown of the physical and chemical properties of the formula when once mixed with water.

For best results, mix dip fresh and dispose of the unused mixture. My purpose in doing this has another reason. I am sure you've experienced the feeling of minor discomfort when a human hair stylist pours cold shampoo on your head after first rinsing it with warm water. The sudden change is shocking, but of course you realize what is being done. The animal you are grooming, however, simply feels the temperature difference, on its whole body.

A more compassionate approach is to warm the shampoo by floating the container in a pot of hot water. This will warm the contents and take the chill off so that the animal will be more comfortable during the bath process. Dip solutions should also be made up of a warm water base for comfort. Since dip is used by gallons a day in most active shops, it is not to be expected that volumes of salvaged dip would be kept warmed.

Conditioner rinses, designed to eliminate static from the coat, and therefore make for better styling, also add softness, and in use help eliminate residual shampoo from the coat. Rinses are applied after the shampoo is rinsed from the coat during the bathing process.

The rinse is applied after being diluted as recommended by the manufacturer and worked into the coat with the hands, allowed to rest for a few minutes, more or less depending upon the final results desired. Generally, a longer treatment will produce a softer coat, which may not be desirable in all breeds. The conditioner rinse is then flushed out of the coat with clear tepid water.

Oil treatments — so-called "Hot Oil" — are designed to eliminate the dry skin condition often produced when a dog has had a severe case of flea or other dermatitis caused by allergy. Additional reason for hot oil use may be after heavy matted coat removal, with subsequent itchy skin associated with same. Dead matted fur saps the skin of natural oils, and close clipper work, which is required to remove the matting, may produce the condition.

Winter months find pets lying next to hot air vents to keep warm. This may also contribute to dry coats, which may benefit from hot oil treatments.

Since there are several different brands on the market, close adherence to the manufacturer's directions is required. Some are multi-step, multi-ingredient formulas. The amount of product must be gauged properly for the breed coat to avoid oversaturation, which can produce a greasy feel, improper for extensive scissor styling.

At least one hot oil treatment that I've used extensively with good results also provides for the direct inclusion of the dip if desired. Both hot oil treatment and parasite killing or preventative dip may be applied at the same time. Naturally, the eyes should be protected with mineral oil, as previously mentioned.

In all cases of wet applications, whether baths, dips, or treatments, extra care should be taken not to allow the liquid to enter the dog's ears, lest it set up a wet warm breeding ground for mites, leading to otitis — a stubborn, often chronic condition that should be avoided at all costs.

Bathing procedure

In addition to all other supplies, arm yourself with a soft bristle brush (the type sold in supermarkets for scrubbing is fine). Choose a fiber bristle, however, since nylon may be too abrasive. A shower spray hose attachment fastened to the faucet will convert any tub for shower bathing.

If a dip is to be given, drop eyes for protection — NOW! The dog is now positioned down in the tub with front feet on the drain board if possible. Be aware that some will not take this position due to obesity, ailing weak rear legs, or arthritis. In these cases simply work the dog with all four feet in the tub, standing on the rubber mat. A leash or chain is now positioned around the dog's neck to prevent jumping, which with slippery feet could produce broken bones if the animal were to hit the floor.

The dog is rinsed with tepid water, starting at the tail end so as to permit it to get used to the water and become aware of the procedure. Be sure to wet the head and face with a quick on-off splash of water from the spray, so as not to cause the dog difficulty in breathing. After thorough wetting, diluted shampoo is now applied by either squirting or spraying on all parts of the dog's anatomy.

The brush is used taking long strokes, with your other hand holding the portion of the body that is being scrubbed. Don't try to do a safe efficient job without holding the animal and giving support to its limbs. When washing the ears, be sure that the opening is covered with your free hand, or plug the ear canal with a piece of absorbent cotton that has been covered with Vaseline. This will form a watertight seal and help prevent ear infections. In the case of long-eared dogs such as Poodles, hold the ear to be washed lying flat in your hand, the underside in your palm, and scrub the upper side using straight up and down motion, not circular, which can snarl the hair. When the upper side is completed, flip the ear over, letting it lie on the neck and back while holding your hand over the opening, pressing the hand down to seal off the ear. Now wash the inside of the ear, the same as the outside.

To wash the head, take a grip on the muzzle by placing the thumb over the top and encircling the muzzle with the fingers, in a grip similar to that which you would use to hold a hammer. Now wash the top of the head taking care not to flush any of the suds and lather down over the eyes. Use the hand holding the muzzle to stroke back, and squeeze off the suds when finished scrubbing.

The same hand grip (muzzle grip) is used to hold the dog when washing the face, exposing one side and then the other by taking a reverse grip to gain access. On one side the thumb is pointing right, and then left for the other. The brush is used stroking down away from the eyes, and with caution not to force suds into the nose. The mouth should be held closed when doing the face, lest the dog consume soap suds which can cause discomfort and illness. Stroke and squeeze off the suds when scrubbing is finished.

After all upper body portions have been scrubbed, wash gently with the brush the underbelly, genitals, anal area, and under the pads of the feet. Scrub the pads thoroughly to remove any sand, dirt and grit, which not only could affect the health of the foot, but which could dull clipper blades if pad shaving were to be done later.

Rinse

All suds and lather are now rinsed, using tepid water. Start at the rear of the dog to allow it to get used to the temperature and pressure of the water. Use a good forceful stream to flush the suds, dirt and possibly insects from the coat and leave it clean. Rinse the ears using the same grip as when scrubbing. The same precautions to avoid water in the ear canals should be taken.

Finally, rinse the head and face in that order, using the same hand controls as previously. The spray must be rinsed on and off over the face to avoid water being inhaled by the dog. Care must be taken not to spray water directly up into the nostrils.

It's a good precaution to hold onto the dog at the neck area at this point to avoid being drenched yourself, if the dog should decide to shake.

The animal is now drained of all rinse water by squeezing firmly on the legs, tail and ears. The body portion is squeezed with the hands until no water runs off.

Dips, conditioners, hot oil treatments, and any other wet applications may now be applied if desired. Remember to protect the eyes with mineral oil, and protect the ears the same as when shampooing. Dips will normally be left on, as will hot oil treatments. Flea shampoos and conditioner rinses will be washed out with a final water rinse after being allowed to take action for several minutes, depending upon the product used.

Fluff dry

Precede fluff drying with a brisk toweling to draw out as much moisture as possible. Proper use of the towel will reduce hot air or forced air drying time, which is desirable.

Start by drying the head, ears and face. This will reduce the dog's desire to shake the water from those areas, and prevent residual dip from being slung into your eyes while drying the dog. Next, towel the body, both top and underbelly and groin areas. Don't forget under the forelegs, and the anal area including the tail. Now grasp a rear leg with the towel in one hand and, using the towel in your grip on the dog, dry the leg and foot pads with both hands at the same time.

Continue fluff drying with an overall light brushing *against the grain.* Use the same steps and control positions as with the initial brushing procedure, but do this very lightly and quickly. At this point your dog should have been made free of any mats and tangles, so just a few long strokes on each side of the body and legs will do. Brush the ears and tail *with the grain.* Brush the head first with, then *against the grain.* Unless the face has a full growth, such as a beard, no brushing is required.

The air stream produced by the dryer is directed onto the coat so that it is blowing *against the grain* if a stand or hand dryer is used. This will tend to lift the coat as it dries and give it the greatest fullness. A brush should be used to assist the process and help speed up the procedure.

Start at the head, brushing *against the grain* and directing the air stream at the base of the hair. The ears are brushed *with the grain,* and the air stream directed freely over them. Protect the ear opening with your hand when fluff drying the inside of the ears. Naturally, you will also protect the eyes from the heat and drying effect of the air. You will have to exert control over the dog to do the head and facial areas, as most dogs don't like to have hot air blowing in these areas.

Continue to work down toward the tail, including it. Remember to brush *against the grain* occasionally on the body. The tail may be brushed *with the grain* until fluffy and dry. Fluff dry the legs last. Brush *against the grain* and adjust the air stream to blow into the coat at the base of the hair shafts.

Short-coated dogs may be cage dried to conserve time. The dog is first lightly brushed all over as before, and then placed into a cage of size large enough to accommodate it. A towel may be draped over the top and side to confine the heat and air volume and cause it to circulate. The dog should be removed every five minutes to be brushed to "fluff" the coat.

The five-minute breaks also prevent overheating the animal in the confined space. Special care should be afforded aged and infantile animals whose lungs may not be able to accept a steady dose of hot air in a confined space. These may be best handled by cage drying until damp dry, then table fluff dry to finish. In any case, a dog should never be placed in a cage to dry and then left unsupervised for any lengthy period. It's not always possible to know if a pet has a chronic heart problem or breathing condition that could be aggravated by excessive hot air dryers.

Forced air dryers that work on a cool air principle are an option that must also be looked at carefully. Since there is no heat in these units, they rely upon a high-velocity air stream to blast the water from the coat. Care must be taken not to direct the air stream in the eyes or ears of tender pups or older animals who are very sensitive, or of any dog who could be injured by same. The wind chill factor is something often overlooked that could also be detrimental. The higher-velocity "no heat dryers" also depend upon rapid evaporation to process the coat to a acceptable dry state. With rapid evaporation you also lower skin temperature. For this reason, I would not recommend using this type equipment on older dogs and puppies.

Shaving foot pads, feet, and pedicuring

All dogs whose coats require regular periodic clipping need to have the hair removed from between the bottoms of the foot pads. This removal is best accomplished with an Oster A5-15 clipper blade. The hair is actually shaved out, and the area left devoid of any hair, clean to the skin.

There may be controversy created by my previous statement, since much has been written on the same subject, with the advice being to "scissor the hair flush with the foot pads." I totally disagree with that procedure, for the following reasons. Most dogs are walked or allowed to run outside. The hair that remains between the pads acts as a magnet to attract chewing gum, cinders and glass, which can bind the hair into a mat, abrade the foot, cut the pads, and cause a condition known as splay foot. When the matting becomes thick enough it causes the foot to spread in a unnatural position, putting pressure and repositioning toe bones other than they should be. The foot and toes spread out, giving unsatisfactory support to the dog. The lump of matted hair alone will act as a stone would in your own shoe. I have removed matted hair from Poodles, Cockers, Lhasas, etc., that was almost as hard as stone, with the poor animal having to suffer to that point.

Matted hair underfoot also can add cause of a nasty chronic condition known as foot fungus, similar to athlete's foot in humans. The mat becomes wet with urine or feces as a result of the dog's being walked repeatedly in the same area to relieve itself. This may be a community area frequented by other dogs as well. The soaked mat, even if only wet with water from the wet grass, provides a moist, warm breeding ground for bacteria, germs, and even parasites.

To complicate matters, when the foot becomes irritated as a result, the dog will bite and lick and also ingest anything that is housed in the matted infected feet. In contrast, of the dogs I have groomed over a 25-year period, fewer than 15 showed evidence of foot infection of any kind. This too is due to taking the extra step of swabbing all shaved feet with antiseptic when completed. To this add the knowledge of the comfort given to the animal, and I am sure you will agree that pad shaving and swabbing is worth the effort.

The procedure may be done with the dog standing on the grooming table or while hanging in a canvas sling jacket designed for the purpose.

Start at the rear of the dog and grasp one foot in the hand not holding the clipper. Hold the foot now by the toes, with your thumb on the bottom of them and fingers on the top. Your grasp will resemble someone trying to pull a pencil from another's hand, and the bottom of the toes will be facing you. The large pad of the foot, sort of equivalent to our own heel, is the starting point in the shaving procedure. Turn the clipper on

Position clipper for nails

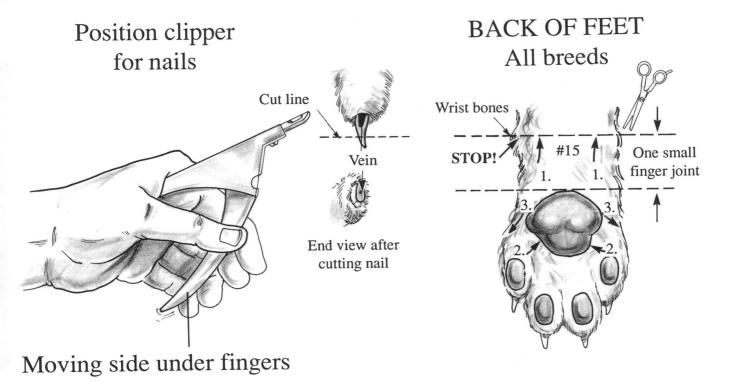

Cut line

Vein

End view after cutting nail

Moving side under fingers

BACK OF FEET All breeds

Wrist bones

STOP! #15 One small finger joint

1. 1.

3. 3.

2. 2.

Front of feet POODLES ONLY

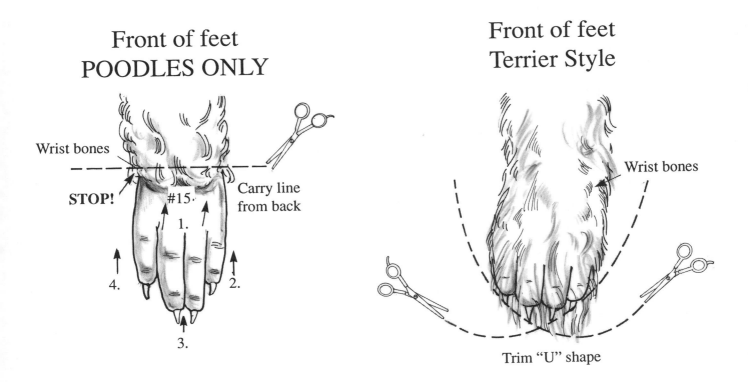

Wrist bones

STOP! #15 Carry line from back

1.

4. 2.

3.

Front of feet Terrier Style

Wrist bones

Trim "U" shape

and place the points of the blade edge on the upper portion of the heel pad at exactly where the hair starts growing. You will at this point shave *against the grain,* up the lower leg above the foot, a distance of about ¾". This is usually equal to the first joint of the average small finger, which may be used to assess the shaved area for proper length.

Do not attempt to shave this area all in one stroke of the clipper. If you do, you probably will shave too high. You must shave a little, check, shave some more, and check until the proper distance is obtained. This area is referred to as the pastern line, having been shaved on the pastern area of the leg.

The next procedure is a bit tricky to position yourself for, but once done, allows for a smooth, quick shaving process in a difficult area. To shave the area between the toe pads, and the heel pad, standing behind the dog, first grasp the outside toe (the left one if you're right-handed), with your thumb and index finger in a pinch grip. Now stretch your middle finger around and over to the inside toe and squeeze it to the side of your index finger. When done properly, you will now have the space between the toes spread open for shaving. The two longer toes in front stay together, side by side.

With the A5-15 blade, shave *against the grain* between the toe pad on one side and the large heel pad. Start at the side of the space. You may have to feel for the starting place if the hair has overgrown the bottom of the foot. Use the full edge of the blade, with the points making contact with the skin very gently. The skin in this area is very thin and tender, and will irritate or cut if excessive pressure is used. A scooping motion must be used to lift the hair so that it will shave off. The motion will be the same as used to scoop a hole out in garden soil.

Always follow through with the clipper in a smooth rocking motion. Do one side completely, then enter the space between the other side toe and heel pad and shave it clean. After the two pad spaces are completed, allow the toes to close and hold the foot in position by holding with your thumb on the shaved pastern line, and your index finger on the side opposite your thumb. The middle, ring, and little fingers will be used to support the foot. From behind the dog, shave *against the grain* across the bottom of all the toe pads, to remove all hair not shaved off previously. This allows the dog's toes to make good contact with the ground, giving it good traction on slippery surfaces such as kitchen floors. The procedure is repeated on all four feet, and is all the shaving required for all breeds except the Poodle, which is more specialized.

Poodle feet are started exactly the same as other breeds and then, continuing from the rear of the foot, shave the side of the foot, starting at the toenail, *against the grain* up to the previously shaved pastern line. This line of shaving is repeated on the other outside toe to the pastern line. Now you will turn the dog, if being done on the table, or walk to the front of the dog, if being supported in a grooming sling.

Facing the front side of the foot, hold the foot in position by grasping the four toes in a pinch hold with the thumb on top, fingers below. At the point where the toes join the upper part of the foot, shave a line *against the grain* up to the same point that was shaved on the outside toes. When done, the whole upper half of the foot should now be shaved clean of hair.

Grasp this newly shaved area, thumb on top, fingers below, to expose and position the lower portion of the foot, the toes. Start at the top of the nails and shave *against the grain* up over the toes to meet and blend in with the previously shaved foot. Use the forefinger of the hand holding the clipper to push up on the hair that is hidden between the toes, and shave it off *against the grain,* same as the toes.

Shaving between the toes is tricky because a thin web of skin connects one toe to another. This web is easily cut if precaution is not taken to avoid it. This is done by grasping the foot the same as the top of the toe shaving grip, thumb on top of area above the toes on the upper part of the foot, and middle finger placed under the web between the toes to be shaved clean. The middle finger is allowed to extend to the edge of the web so as to protect it from injury. The other fingers are used to maintain a firm grip on the foot.

The thumb is now used to press between the upper junction of the toes, as the middle finger presses up. This combined opposing pressure spreads the toes apart, permitting the A5-15 blade to enter *against the grain* and shave between safely. As the blade nears the junction point between the toes, scoop out to one side or the other to get a complete clean shave in that area. When all toes are finished, repeat for the other feet.

This is a frustrating process to learn, but must be mastered if you are to be able to safely shave feet Poodle style.

Clipping the nails

After the foot shaving operation has been completed, either pad shaving only or complete Poodle style feet, it's time to clip the nails.

Canine nails differ from human nails in that canine nails contain a nervous system and blood supply in a pulpy core. This is called the quick. Nails improperly clipped can cause a variety of situations leading to misery for the animal.

Clip the nail too short and the animal suffers pain. Leave the nail too long, and it will also suffer from catching them in loop type carpeting, in their own coat when scratching, and some when they poke their paws through the front door mail slot in an effort to see the postman. As the foot is withdrawn, the mail slot flap acts as a trap and locks down on long curved nails. The dog panics and pulls harder in an effort to gain its freedom and sometimes rips a nail partially out of its toe, or at least breaks one short into the quick. If undetected quickly, the toe may become infected and require amputation. This simply because the nails were not clipped short enough, if at all.

Not all dogs will require as frequent a nail clipping as others. Heavy dogs who are walked a lot, outside dogs, diggers, and those professionally groomed on less than a four-week basis may not require this service, except for certain nails that do not contact

NAIL TRIMMING AND THE BLOOD SUPPLY (KWIK) OF THE NAILS OF THE DOG

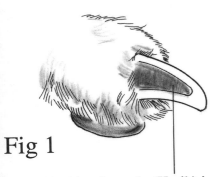

Fig 1

The blood supply (Kwik) in
a short nail.

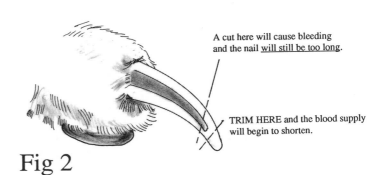

A cut here will cause bleeding
and the nail will still be too long.

TRIM HERE and the blood supply
will begin to shorten.

Fig 2

The blood supply gets
longer as the nail grows.

Fig 3

Clip or file a small amount off
a long nail every few days
and the blood supply will recede.

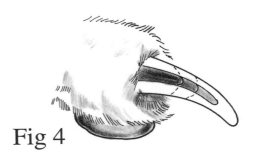

Fig 4

As the nail shortens so
does the blood supply.

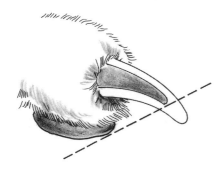

Fig 5

Only when a nail is
kept short can it be trimmed
without bleeding. The same
cut made on the long nail
in Figure two would have caused bleeding.

Fig 6

A properly trimmed nail

the ground. These high-positioned nails are attached to their own pad just above the foot, on the inside of the leg. They are called dewclaws. If not kept short, they tend to curl around in a circular fashion. Sometimes they will curl around and pierce the flesh, actually entering it, creating a wound that is seen when the nail is clipped and extracted. Oriental breeds, such as the Pekingese, seem to be prone to this problem.

Spreading of the toes, creating splay foot, a painful walking condition, can also be attributed to overgrown, curved, neglected nails.

The instrument most used to clip the canine nail is called a guillotine nail clipper. There are also scissor types, side cutters I have employed when clipping the nails that can't be engaged with the traditional guillotine type. These are the recurved nails that don't offer an end to slip the guillotine over. Although nail clippers are available in a variety of sizes, a medium size tool will work for all breeds. If extra-large dogs are to be frequently serviced, a large clipper would give more leverage in the clipping procedure and therefore would be advantageous.

The nail clipping procedure is the one that is least liked by the average dog, even more so than the bath, which in my experience has actually seemed to be enjoyed by most dogs rather than disliked. Best cooperation is received from the dog when you've mastered the procedure so that it can be done quickly but accurately, moving from one nail to the next without hesitation.

If a grooming sling is used, take a standing position behind the dog, If working on the table, your position would be standing in front, back, or on the side of the dog. In either case, be advised that a muzzle may have to be used to prevent groomer injury in the event the dog turns aggressive.

The toe of the nail to be clipped is held in a pinch grip with the thumb and forefinger, while the rest of the foot is controlled with the balance of the fingers and palm.

The nail clipper is held so that the moveable arm of the tool is under the fingers and the stationary arm rests in the palm against the heel of the hand. Although this tool is often pictured in advertising in the reverse position, it should not be held this way, since doing so will cause the tool to dip toward the foot. This will engage more nail than is desirable and clip shorter than planned. If the tool is held pointed to the left (or right if you're left-handed), it will have less tendency to crush the nail, causing pain until the blade finally cuts all the way through. The way most often depicted is with the cutter portion pointing up. This causes the tool to clip through the widest front-to-back portion of the nail. Holding it sideways, to the right or left, allows you to clip through the narrow side-to-side portion without the crushing effect.

Start clipping a small amount from the end of the nail and continue until a dark spot, the quick, appears in the center of black nails, or a pink one in white nails. Should the nail start to bleed, this is indication that you have clipped too deep and have hit the quick. This may be avoided by clipping smaller portions, and checking the cut end after each clip of 1/16".

When the spot appears, stop! The method usually employed to stop the bleeding is the use of a blood vessel constrictor called iron subsulfate. Alum-sulphate and electric cauteries are also methods sometimes used to stop the occasional bleeder. These products are readily available under a variety of trade names.

To stop the flow quickly, remove all tools from your hands and press a small amount of the constrictor into the end of the nail, pressing in tightly with a twisting motion of your thumb. You must pack the powder in below the surface lest it chip off and start bleeding again when the dog walks on the paving.

Each nail, including the dewclaws, should be clipped square across the width of the nail so as not to produce sharp angled edges that can scratch or cut the owners, furniture, stockings, etc. Holding the clipper at right angles will solve the problem. After the nails are clipped, the sharp edges can be softened with a Nail File. I, however, always simply advise owners to take the dog for a walk on the pavement, since many dogs are greatly annoyed by the vibration of filing and create havoc during the process.

Trimming the feet

Tools required are the slicker brush and straight pointed scissor. The way the feet are trimmed is dependent upon the way both the body and the feet will be styled.

Terrier breeds' feet are trimmed by grasping the toes from behind the dog, holding with the thumb on the toe pads and the fingers on the top of the toes in a pinch grip. The slicker brush is then used *with the grain* over the pastern shaved line area to bring down all uneven hair. Now, from the outside of the foot, insert the point of the scissor under the overhanging hair; when fully inserted, hold the scissor edge at a right angle, 90 degrees to the foot, and trim straight across. You should produce a clean line with the hanging wisps of hair; otherwise, retrim until neat.

The foot is trimmed by grasping the foot from behind the dog. At the previously trimmed pastern area, hold the thumb at the back and fingers over the front. The paw is positioned with the fingers so that it is slightly elevated and you can see the toe pads easily while standing behind the foot. With the opposite hand, slicker brush the hair on the top of the foot, from behind the dog, *with the grain,* bringing all long hair down past the edge of the foot. Slide the fingers of the hand holding the foot down over the front of the foot, over onto the toes supporting the whole paw in position.

The pointed scissor is now used to trim around the foot close to the nails in a lazy V shape, rounding the edge at the tip of the middle toes' nails. The trim line should look clean and sharp, with no stray hairs.

Care must be taken not to return to the leg with the trimming procedure. This would accent the foot, making it look more like a Poodle foot style. Simply trim from one nail to the next in a lazy V shape.

Shaved Poodle feet are trimmed by holding the foot starting from behind. Brush *with the grain* at the previously shaved pastern line. The pointed scissor is inserted from the side under the overhanging hair and trimmed straight across the same as the Terrier breeds, at right angles. Using this trim line as a guide, trim the right and left side of that foot in a continuous line. Remember to brush *with the grain* each time prior to scissor trimming the lines.

Now step to the front of the foot, facing it. Brush the shaved pastern line overhang *with the grain.* Using the trimmed side lines as a guide, trim the front line. Keep the scissor at right angles at all times. You will find this easier to do if you elevate the leg so that it is in a position parallel to the floor. A cleaner, sharper line will result from keeping the lower scissor blade point on the skin when trimming. When completed, the Poodle trim line will represent a neat even cuff just above the foot joint. This area would be similar to your own wrist.

Poodles, whose feet are not shaved between the toes, would be trimmed the same as Terriers, plus extra trimming on the top of the unshaven foot. Complete the trim as previously described for Terriers and then turn and face the front of the foot.

Now brush lightly *against the grain* to raise and fluff the hair over the foot. Begin at the outside of the foot and trim a smooth, compact rounded mound over the top of the foot. Trim only the hair that is standing up. Don't attempt to trim the hair when it lies down or you will expose the toes and the nails. A proper job will be obvious, as will an improper one.

At Pennsylvania School of Dog Grooming, I refer to this foot style as "natural trimming" because it more readily resembles the Poodle's foot in natural growth than when shaved in Poodle style. With the return-to-basics movement, this has become increasingly more popular.

This method of Poodle foot styling is a perfect solution for those dogs whose feet are so sensitive that foot shaving between the toes is traumatic for them, and almost impossible to do without restraints. Remember, the health of the animal should always be given first precedent over style. The "natural" style satisfies the needs of the animal perfectly and keeps the feet neat.

Foot swabbing

After the feet have been shaved, I have always taken the extra time to swab the shaved areas with alcohol. Just as after-shave lotion has an antiseptic and soothing effect on shaved human skin, so does the application of alcohol to a dog's feet. In the course of shaving, it is near impossible to avoid tiny abrasions. The feet are ever exposed to paving, stones, broken glass, bits of metal, and bacteria. Some feet may have a tiny scab that isn't noticed until hair is shaved off, with the scab.

No matter how careful the groomer, sometimes the blade edge will scrape the tissue between the toes of a dog that suddenly kicks or struggles during the shaving procedure. The abrasion may be so slight as not to be even noticed by the naked eye, but it's there. By making it a habit to swab all feet as a regular prophylactic procedure, the dog is given an extra measure of a chance at good foot health.

An absorbent cotton ball is saturated with 70% isopropyl alcohol and wiped over and between all shave areas of the feet, *with the grain.* Wiping *against the grain* will leave a residue of cotton particles clinging to the hair, which is undesirable and is detrimental when nails are to be polished on Poodles. The alcohol has the added benefit of removing any oily film from the nails prior to polishing, and it also dries rapidly, leaving the crevices between the toes dry. This also helps in the prevention of fungus infections. The rapid evaporation of alcohol has a cooling effect that the dogs seem to appreciate after feet are shaved. Other antiseptic solutions that contain water as the main vehicle should be avoided. These would include, but are not limited to, Listerine and hydrogen peroxide. The latter could also bleach out the coat, turning it a sickly unnatural color.

Nail polishing (Poodles only, please!)

It is possible to polish the nails on any breed, at the request of the client. This procedure, however, is best reserved for the most ornately styled canine, the Poodle. Naturally it would be done only on one whose feet have been shaved clean. Dog nail polish, which comes in a grand variety of colors, has a rapid dryer in it, and some contain epoxy to create a harder finished surface. It is important, therefore, to avoid excessive brushing in the application of the polish to each nail. Three to four strokes at maximum are what is required to eliminate the possibility of streaks and brush marks on the finished polished surface. Start by standing the dog on all four feet on the table, or support in the grooming sling. The sling makes the job even easier since all four feet hang straight down for easy access, and remove the possibility of polish being smeared by the dog's moving.

Start with a rear foot. Dip the brush into the polish bottle and get a good amount on it without removing too much excess as you withdraw it from the bottle. The ideal is enough to be able to polish all nails on one foot with one brush load. Take each nail individually by holding the toe, looking at it from the front of the foot. Start with an outside nail and stroke on the outside of it, then the inside, then the top. Make a definite stroke, putting enough pressure on the brush so that the bristles bend in the polish application. Remember, strive for three or four strokes maximum per nail. Move quickly from one to the other until all nails except the dewclaw nail are polished on one foot. If working on the table, place the foot down and hold it in position until you have picked up the other rear foot.

The reason we start with the rear foot is to avoid being pawed at with a newly polished front foot while attempting to do the rear. You could also more easily smear from foot nails that are still wet, when reaching to do the rear nails. If working in the sling, simply place the foot with nails just polished in the relaxed hanging position and repeat the process on the next rear foot. Do not release the foot after polishing and allow it to spring back into position on its own. Place it there, or it may smear on the other leg. Since you've previously swabbed the shaved feet prior to polishing, you shouldn't encounter any loose hairs on the nails that would get stuck to the nails.

If a hair or two does interfere, don't touch it until the polish is dry, when it will easily snap off without smearing the polish all over the foot or your fingers. Two minutes after the last nail was polished, touch it on the bottom, the cut edge, with your finger. If it seems dry, touch it on the inside side of the nail. If dry, you may now assume all nails are dry. Doing it this way, you avoid smearing the top show portion of the nail if the nail is still wet. At this point, your Poodle-style feet are complete and fancy.

Clipping the body

Before the body can be clipped, you must first realize that it consists of various parts that must be dealt with individually. The control that must be established over the animal can be maintained only if you are able to manipulate it without causing discomfort. An uncomfortable dog will not respond in the manner you require to be able to perform the clipping operation safely.

The blades used are sharp pointed instruments with wide spaces between the teeth. It is critical that areas of protruding tissue be protected lest they enter between the blade tooth spaces and cause serious injury to the animal. In operation, the blade tooth points must come in contact with the skin. This is what produces a smooth clipped coat. If the points are held away from the skin, the hair will catch in the blade, and the hair will pull and be chewed between the blade parts. This can produce a jammed blade. If the problem is not quickly recognized, and force is attempted to move the blade through the coat, it may bruise the animal, or worse, produce a wound. Either way you would have lost control due to not having observed an important instruction, of which there are many.

These will now be related to you, and they will coincide with the body clipping chart contained elsewhere in this book. Each instruction has a definite purpose, and should be adhered to even if you are not able to initially comprehend that purpose. With application and practice, eventually all will become crystal clear.

The length attained when clipping the body will be dependent upon the blade used. Each blade has its own special characteristics and uses. To know what results to expect, you must first get to know the blades you are to use. When speaking of the amount of coat left after clipping, we refer to the fullness. When using Oster professional clipping equipment, the blade that leaves the most "fullness" is the A5-4. This blade differs from the others that will be described in that it is the thickest of all the blades the company manufactures. It is this thickness that provides greater distance between the widely spaced, pointed "comb" edge and "cutter" or moving portion of the blade set.

In use, all blades will operate best when the points of the "comb" edge are brought into direct contact with the skin. The blade then measures from the skin back to the points of the "cutter" blade and clips at that position. The resultant length that remains is the "fullness" attained. The A5-4 blade will produce a fullness of from 5/8" to 3/4"; the variable measurement will depend upon the position of the hair when the clipping is done, and also the texture of the hair. If the hair is brushed "up," *against the grain* prior to clipping, it will clip shorter. It will also clip more evenly, since the hair is put into a standing position, more evenly stationed than if left lying down in a natural state. Because of this, we always clip *with the grain* after brushing *against the grain*.

Hair with a coarse texture will clip leaving a shorter fullness than soft hair. This is because coarse hair resists the touch of the clipper blade. It just tends to stand there until the blade cuts it off. Hair that is soft will start to lie down when contacted by the blade. The partially down position of the hair causes the blade to pass over it until it will cut it, leaving it longer. This same principle will apply to all blades used.

The A5-5 blade will clip from 3/8" to 1/2" fullness and is referred to as a medium fullness clipping blade. It too has the hump on its back that the A5-4 blade has, and is the only other blade that does. It can now be realized that the "humpback" blades are used exclusively where an amount of fullness is desired in excess of 3/8". All of the other blades listed in this work will leave a lesser amount of fullness because they do not have the thickness that the humpback blades do.

The A5-7 blade will clip from 3/16" to 1/4" fullness, and is the most dangerous blade in the set to use. The ultra-sharp long points, and wide spaces between points, can easily engage and cut animal tissue. Strict safety practice must be employed when using this blade if injury is to be avoided. I don't know how any groomer of Poodles, Lhasa Apsos, Shih-tzus, and other long-coated dogs could stay in business if this blade were not available. This would seem contradictory, but the reason for it is the coat condition. More than 50% of all the long-haired glamour breeds at some time in their life will require their coats "cut down" because of extreme matting due to neglect. The matting will be so severe that a comb will not be able to be passed through it. Even after hours of brushing it would not be possible to comb this type of matted "felted" coat.

The A5-4 and A5-5 blades, with their thick comb edge, can't pass through it either. The only solution is to remove the coat at the source of the problem. The heavy mat is at the skin line, so that is where it must be removed.

The A5-7 blade has points that will wedge under and split the matting. The spacing between the comb teeth allows the matted hair to enter (flesh, too, if you are not careful), and the cutter portion then finishes the job. It would also be possible to use a lesser fullness blade. This would, however, leave the animal completely devoid of hair, with no protection for the skin, which has become sensitized due to the closeness of the procedure.

The A5-7 blade will remove matting as thick as a carpet. I have never come across a situation that this workhorse blade couldn't handle. The very aggressive construction of the A5-7 is what makes it so useful. It may also be used for quick clipping of coats in good condition when about 1/4" fullness is desired, as in the "Beachcomber" summer clip style. The spacing of the A5-7 is so wide that it can easily channel the dense hair to cut it.

The A5-8 1/2 blade is the blade of choice when a short length over bony anatomy is desired. Areas such as the face, skull, and base of the tail will present a problem that can be easily solved when the A5-8 1/2 is employed.

Attempts to use the A5-8 1/2 blade where you would use the A5-7 on matted coats would result in constant jamming and much needed force to try to pass it through the coat. The safety of the animal would be jeopardized.

When a short length of hair is desired on the dog's face, the A5-8½ blade is perfect. This assumes that the face isn't matted, but in good combable condition. You can obtain the same closeness as the A5-7 without the dangerous sharp wedge points and spaces to contend with near the eyes, nose and mouth.

The A5-8½ is also invaluable when less than ⅜" fullness is desired, when a very sparse, straight hair coated dog is to be styled. The A5-7 either would leave a choppy effect on such a coat, or would skim over it without removing anything. This is because the spacing of the A5-7 is so wide that it can't properly channel the sparse hair to cut it. The A5-8½ blade is the blade of choice when a short length over bony anatomy is desired. Areas such as the face, skull, and base of the tail will present a problem that can be easily solved when the A5-8½ is employed.

Although there are many other blades also manufactured by Oster, Sunbeam, Wahl, Sears, etc., those mentioned above are all that are required for the clipping procedures.

Areas of the body requiring much closer work with almost total hair removal are referred to as shaved areas. The most used blade of all those available is the A5-15. This is the blade that the feet were shaved with. When a shaved appearance is desired, the A5-15 is the blade to use. It is a multi-use blade in that it may be used on various parts of the body very effectively. Unlike the clipping blades, the A5-15 is usually used *against the grain*. The clipping blades are almost always used *with the grain*. When a shaved look is desired, but the animal's skin is sensitive to closer shaving, the A5-15 companion blade A5-10 may be used.

The A5-10 is also a shaving blade. It would appear to be identical to the A5-15, since the difference is so slight. A novice will have to look at the blade number, which appears on the comb portion at the bottom right corner. When compared to the A5-15 blade, the A5-10's cutter teeth will set back further from the comb edge than will the A5-15. It is this slight setback that makes the difference. It allows for a small fraction more hair to remain after the shaving operation is completed. It must be remembered when using this blade that this additional length is intentional; excessive restroking over the previously shaved area, in an attempt to obtain a "cleaner look," will merely tend to irritate the animal, defeating the purpose.

Sometimes when using the A5-10 in the groin area, you may find it difficult to "pick up" the hair. The blade seems to skim right over it. In this situation, it would be best to switch to an A5-15 blade rather than continue to stroke and restroke over and over the area. The attempt would prove more irritating then if the A5-15 were used initially.

When working with a shaving blade of any number, the following precautions should be taken: Always be sure that all comb edge points make skin contact at the same time. This will avoid the sharp pointed corners from digging into the skin and injuring sensitive areas such as the groin. Always check the blade temperature prior to shaving. Place the blade against the inside of your forearm. You will respond faster to the temperature there than if tested in the palm of the hand. Be aware that extensive shaving can produce heat great enough to burn tender tissues. A prime example might be when shaving Poodle style feet. The amount of time required for this operation will

CLIPPING SEQUENCE

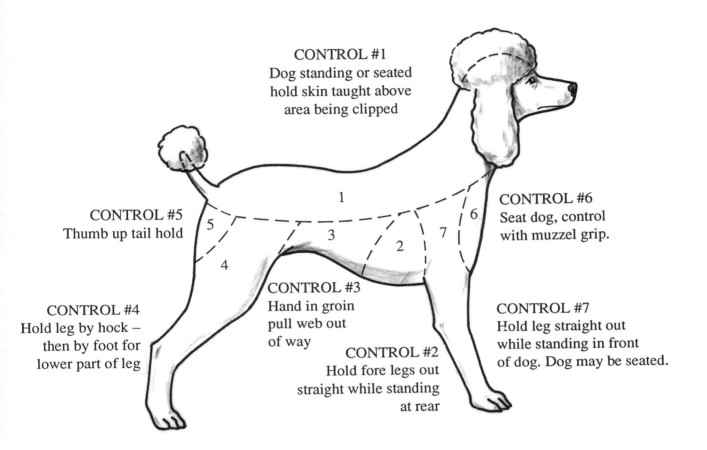

CONTROL #1
Dog standing or seated
hold skin taught above
area being clipped

CONTROL #6
Seat dog, control
with muzzel grip.

CONTROL #5
Thumb up tail hold

CONTROL #4
Hold leg by hock –
then by foot for
lower part of leg

CONTROL #3
Hand in groin
pull web out
of way

CONTROL #2
Hold fore legs out
straight while standing
at rear

CONTROL #7
Hold leg straight out
while standing in front
of dog. Dog may be seated.

FIRST CLIPPING RUN
Whole body brushed against the grain (A/G)

SECOND CLIPPING RUN
Body is brushed A/G and clipped by sections.

always heat up an A5-15 blade, unless it is periodically cooled down, or the blade changed.

Several products are available to reduce the heat generated. Oster Kool Lube, in a pressure spray can, will cool down and also lubricate the blade with just a few close short spray bursts. These products should also be used on body clipping blades that overheat in order to prevent excess wear of the blades. As the heat increases, the metal expands, causing greater friction. The blade parts tend to bind without lubrication, increasing the strain on all blade parts and also the linkage and motor. Blade cooldown protects not only the animal, but your equipment as well.

Other shaving-type blades are available for "setting patterns." These are shave lines of various widths used for styling specific patterns on Poodles. The A5-8/8 blade shaves a line one inch wide and slightly closer than an A5-15 blade. This blade should not be used to shave Poodle feet. It would seem to a novice that it would be ideal for Poodle feet, due to its small size. Be forewarned that great damage may be done if used for that procedure. The narrow width of the A5-8/8 allows more pressure to unconsciously be exerted on sensitive tissue, and the closer cutter to comb edge will abrade and cut the thin tightly stretched skin of the feet. For the same reasons and more, never use these styling blades around the loin of the dog. More detailed instruction on the use of pattern styling blades will be given later in this work.

Although there are many more blades manufactured, I have never found it necessary to use more than the basic seven described. It would be advantageous to become fully familiar and proficient in the use of these before trying to justify the use of any additional.

Actual body clipping

Now that you have a general idea of what the various blades will do, we can discuss the actual body clipping operation. The exact same hand controls that are used to brush and comb the dog are used to clip it.

Stand the dog on the grooming table facing away from you and instruct it to "stay!" Referring to our brushing, combing, and clipping sequence chart, we now start with area 1. First brush *against the grain* to lift the hair into position. The clipper is held in the hand with the blade points down, gripping the tool as though it were a hammer. The clipping will be done by pulling the clipper as you hold the blade points in contact with the skin at a 30-degree angle. This last statement can't be overemphasized. Do it properly and you'll have no problem obtaining a even smooth clip. In addition to the proper angle, tension must be maintained on the skin to stretch it, and avoid running the blade points into wrinkled flesh.

The hand not holding the clipper is used to grasp the skin starting at the neck area to stretch it toward the head. The clipper is pulled in the opposite direction over the taut skin for a distance of about 4″-6″. As each small section is clipped, the control hand moves to a virgin area to stretch it taut as the clipper is moved into position to clip it.

Each section of the body is controlled after brushing it, as described previously for combing. Instead of the comb, the clipper is used to stroke through the coat to clip it. Strong verbal as well as physical control may be required to keep the dog in position to avoid injuring it as the clipping proceeds. It is strongly advised that the novice move step by step, in numerical order, while referring to the clipping chart until memorized.

Key points to remember

Due to the risk factor of using sharp instruments on live animals, the following steps and precautions should be taken when clipping the various body areas.

AREA 1 (THE BACK AND SIDES): Be sure to hold the coat stretched toward the head as you clip with the grain; this will prevent blade points from catching in skin folds, producing abrasion or cut injury. Exert caution when you start the clip at the base of the ears. This area is frequently matted. Due to its location, it is seldom properly brushed by the owner. The wearing of a collar that is constantly shifting back and forth can cause this area to swirl. A good grip, voice command "Stay," and short positive blade strokes while holding the ears out of the way are required to make a proper start. Don't rush it. Work from one side to the other 4″-6″ at a time until the base of the tail is reached.

AREA 2: When the forelegs are stretched forward, a web of taut skin may be felt at the pit of the foreleg. This web will be greater or lesser in size depending upon the dog. Great care should be exercised when clipping this section not to clip forward and under the pit of the foreleg as the web may be engaged by the blade, producing severe injury. Be sure to clip halfway under the chest from this area position. Do not clip more than halfway back toward the rear legs when doing Area 2, since the stretch obtained by extending the front legs is not effective for more than half the body. Keeping the foreleg up at a 45-degree angle will prevent the dog from lying down when clipping this area.

AREA 3 (THE LOIN): I cannot express enough the caution needed on this easily injured portion of the dog. A long web of skin is found at the upper front portion where leg meets abdomen at the loin. When clipping this area, be sure to keep this web of skin tightly pulled back with the finger in a pistol grip, the same as when combing. The width of the space between the comb edge of most body blades will allow the skin to enter and result in severe injury. Because this area is usually overgrown with hair, it will not be seen, and must be felt.

AREA 4 (THE REAR LEGS): Located above the hock on the rear of the leg is the Achilles tendon, also called the hamstring. There is no real protection for this area afforded by nature. If the tendon is cut all the way through, it will cripple the dog. As with the loin web, the tendon will easily enter the comb edge of most blades. To avoid cutting it, you must not stroke your blade directly behind and across the tendon. The blade should be angled out at 45 degrees to this edge from both outside and inside the leg, and the hair will be clipped at the point where the blade crosses. Any unclipped portion may easily be trimmed with the shears.

The hock bone must also be carefully approached. Not only could the flesh be easily lacerated by the points of the blade, the bone could also be cracked or chipped if struck. Dogs frequently will want to pull up on the legs when clipping. A firm grip on the leg plus awareness is required to avoid painful injury. The A5-7 blade can be especially deadly on the hamstring and the hock.

AREA 5 (SIDE OF ANUS AND BACK OF HIPS): Never clip directly over the anus! The reasons are obvious. Less obvious are the testicles on the males and the sometimes protruding vulva on females. This area must be clipped with strong control exerted to avoid serious injury to genitals, hocks and hamstring tendon. The dog's major defense of the anal area is to seat itself quickly.

If your control (thumb pointed up with hand grasp around the tail) is not strong enough, here's what may happen. You're clipping with the blade points pointing down, toward the table. Let's assume this procedure is being done with an A5-7 blade. The dog suddenly decides to sit to avoid the annoyance of having a clipper blade stroked over his rear. You lose your grip on the tail, the legs fold with the blade coming directly down from behind onto the hamstrings or hocks. The full weight of the dog on the clipper may drive the blade into the legs.

Here's how to counter this possibility before it happens. Keep the elbow of the hand holding the tail down at your side, never pointed out to the left or right. This will give you the leverage to resist the sudden weight that may be dropped on it. Of course, you must keep your grasp tense in preparation for the dog's move.

To avoid injury to the genitals, never clip other than straight down on Area 5, and only after feeling for protrusions, which you will avoid by clipping on the side of them.

AREA 6 (THE CHEST): The dog could be clipped in this area while standing, but this is risky. A seated dog is less apt to move. It must first stand before it can turn around. This gives you a measure of warning. A seated dog whose head is elevated in a control grip is more comfortable than one in control grip that is standing. His neck doesn't have to be bent as far, making it easier to breathe and swallow. Better cooperation will give you better control. Clip slowly over the chest since some dogs will have a protruding breastbone that will be injured if struck by a fast moving blade. Other dogs have skin folds at the throat and chest area that can catch and cut if clipped too fast. This problem is not as great a risk as the former, but it is a caution that should be observed.

AREA 7 (THE FRONT LEGS): The dog should be seated for best control. Normal grip would be holding the foot, thumb over toes. If the dog is uncooperative and pulls hard as you attempt to clip the legs, take the following grip. Grasp above the foot holding the lower foreleg. Clip the upper portions of the leg outside and inside as required by the style. Reposition your grip to a grasp just above the elbow, and then clip the lower leg area. This method gives you good firm control and prevents a strong animal from pulling your own hand onto the clipper blade. Provide the same caution when working at the elbow as you would at the stifle. Never clip directly on top of and behind it when standing in front of the dog. If the dog were to pull the leg back at that time it would injure the pit area, elbow or both.

At this point the basic body clip would be finished. With certain variations, we can now alter the basic style.

The Kennel clip

This method of styling originated many years ago. Dogs would be utility-clipped for a stay in the kennel, hence the term "kennel clipped." This is the least stylish method of clipping and is the easiest for the owner to maintain. The total body and legs are clipped to one length. This clip may be done with any of the body blades depending upon the amount of fullness desired. If in fact the least amount of maintenance is desired, a Kennel clip done with an A5-7 blade will do the job and still leave a hair covering on the dog. This is really what most owners want when they request that the dog be shaved. Shaving the whole body of a dog not used to it may produce problems. It should be done only when the dog can be protected from the sun, and from itself.

Many dogs will rub themselves raw on the ground or on carpeting after a close shave. Certainly, long-coated breeds that usually do not receive regular clipping should not be shaved. For low maintenance, a good A5-7 kennel will do fine, without the potential problems.

When styling a Kennel clip, all of the precautions previously mentioned must be observed. This style puts all areas at risk due to the closeness of the styling, and often due to the use of the A5-7 blade.

The Puppy clip

More stylish and requiring more owner maintenance is the Puppy clip. This may be done with any of the body blades, but the blades of choice are the A5-4 and A5-5. All body areas would be clipped the same as previously described except for the legs, Areas 4 and 7.

The body clipping should preserve the hair at the front point of the shoulder so the hair may be blended into the top of the leg. The same is done at the back of the hip bone, either side of the anus.

The legs, both front and back, would remain wide in appearance by clipping the outside and inside planes only. The front and back edges of the legs remain unclipped, to be trimmed with scissors later.

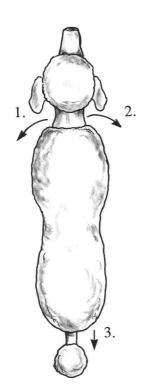

PUPPY CLIP
with shaved
neck line #15

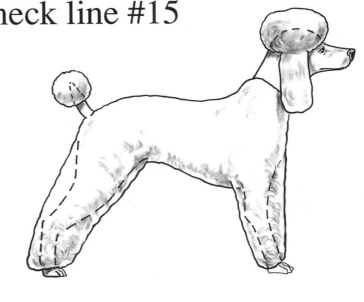

KENNEL

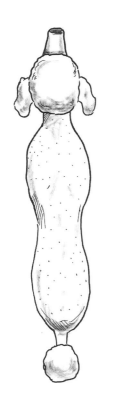

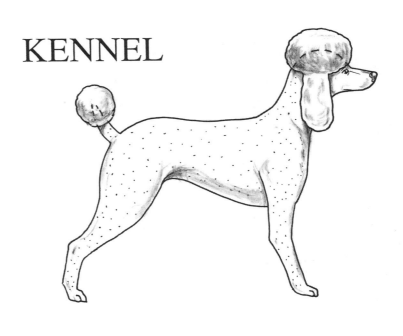

Body clipping: second run

Each body that is clipped should be done twice. The first clipping will remove the bulk of the hair, matting, and overgrowth. The style or pattern will be established, but not refined. When clipped prior to bathing, the first run will reduce the amount of coat to be dried and help speed up the drying process. It is wise, therefore, to clip the first run before bathing whenever possible. There will be situations where it won't be possible to wait to clip before bathing, such as a heavily flea-infested animal. To clip such a dog prior to giving it a flea-killing bath is to invite infestation of the shop, other dogs, and possibly the groomer.

The second clipping body run is done the same as the first, but with more ease. The shorter, cleaner, unmatted coat offers less resistance to the clipper. The second run is a more comfortable procedure because of this, hence better cooperation from the dog. Be sure to brush each section *against the grain,* same as the first run prior to clipping. When done properly, the body will have an even length established in the style desired.

Trimming the body

The use of the groomer's scissor is one of the most difficult procedures for the average student of grooming to master. Few people need to be taught how to open and close them. The difficult thing to learn is where to use them on the dog's body, how much to trim off, and in what area. To ease the problem, I have established basic rules to be followed, which if done will take the mystery out of the "secrets of trimming."

The tools used in trimming range in price from a few dollars to hundreds of dollars for ultrafine instruments. As with any equipment, I have never found it necessary to go overboard in expense in order to obtain satisfying tools. The Double Duck or the Oster 7½″ curved blunt tip Groomer Scissor is what I personally have used for two decades. I have successfully trained hundreds of students at Pennsylvania School of Dog Grooming to trim with this equipment, which is in the $25 price range.

The variety of scissors available is as large as the variance in price: long, short, wide, narrow, pointed, blunt, and each acclaimed for the purpose of their design. Many times a novice will purchase a large variety of equipment. They find later, as they become more accomplished, that just a certain few are all they use or need. For body work, the curved scissor will be used with the blunt tip pointing away from the dog.

Trim the dog's body after the second run has been completed. At this time the dog has gotten a bath, is dry, and should be mat-free. Even so, you will still have to use the slicker to position the hair for trimming.

Start by brushing the hind leg *against the grain* with the dog facing away from you. This is done to lift the coat into position. Next, brush the same leg edge cross grain, so that the hair stands out away from and behind the rear leg. The Puppy clip style attempts to achieve a fuller, straighter-appearing leg, even though the leg has a natural angle formed by the hock joint. To overcome this unpleasing "dogleg" look, the trim line is initiated at the rear hip bone area, and a straight line is trimmed down sighting the hock at the other end of the line. Remember to keep the scissor held in the hand with the blunt tips pointing away from the leg. This will help prevent injury and error in the trimming.

After the line is trimmed as straight as possible, use the slicker to sweep the whole line to the right side of the leg. Trim the newly established line on the edge so that it is straight and compact, free of wispy edges. Now, with the slicker, sweep the hair to the left side of the leg. Assuming that you started with the right rear leg, the line that now requires trimming will be on the inside. It must be trimmed by inserting the scissor between the legs with the leg lifted and held almost parallel to the table.

By trimming the sweep lines, you are actually taking the corner off the edges. This will produce a rounded edge, which is desirable.

The front edge of the right rear leg is next. Brush it *against the grain* and then cross grain to stroke all the hair out and into position. Trim as you did before, but now sight your line on the stifle joint. You will trim within ¼″ of the stifle if you've used an A5-4 or within ⅛″ if an A5-5 was used on the body. This line will be trimmed straight down toward the foot. Do not follow the natural contour of the leg. Where the leg curves in just below the stifle is where you must allow a large quantity of hair to remain to fill in that contour. When properly done, the leg will now appear straight when viewed from the side.

With the slicker, sweep the hair both right and left, and trim as previously. Always keep a check on your progress by occasionally placing the leg down to check the appearance. Throughout the trimming procedure, keep the blunt tip scissor curved away from the body.

When the right rear leg is finished, repeat the process on the left rear leg. Remember to do this while standing behind the dog.

The front legs are trimmed with the dog facing you. Hold the paw of the left leg and slicker it *against the grain* and then cross grain to lift and extend the hair into trimming position. Now sight on the elbow. This is the point at which your trimming will be closest. The hair is then trimmed along the back of the leg on an angle until the same length at the pastern of the back leg is attained on the back of the front leg.

Sweep the leg with the slicker as you did with the rear legs. Then repeat the same total process on the other leg and the leg trimming portion of the procedure will be finished. These are the major lines in the Puppy clip.

The "high spots" refers to those areas that cannot be efficiently clipped with the blade. They may be bumps or lumps such as tumor areas, dewclaws, wisps under the tail on each side of the anus, or shave lines where they meet the fullness of the coat. These are easily reached with a scissor and should be trimmed off neatly so that there is no distraction from the smooth flowing line when viewing from all angles.

A high spot not so easily reached are the pits under the forelegs. Each side requires a separate approach.

Start with the dog's right front foreleg and take an encircling hand grasp high above the elbow with your left hand, and hold it. With your right hand, using your thumb and index finger, reach high up under the pit and with a pinch grip grasp the unclipped hair and pull down and out in front of the leg. Now slightly release your left hand grasp, and with the thumb and index finger of your left hand still holding the encircled leg, take a pinch grip on the flesh behind the hair that is being extended with the right hand. Release the grip on the hair being held by the right hand. You now have the dog in control with your left hand grasp, and also are safely extending the hair for trimming. You are holding the flesh, not the hair, therefore you can't injure the dog since you will be trimming forward of your grip. Never hold the hair by the ends and trim behind them. In doing so you stretch the flesh out away from the body without your fingers protecting the flesh. This incorrect way eventually will lead to a serious injury, cutting off a piece of skin or flesh.

To trim the "height spots" under the dog's left pit, you must take the same grip with the left hand from in front of the right leg, above the elbow. The hair will now be extended with the right hand pinch grip from behind the leg and trimmed as before. When holding the flesh it may be rolled back and forth between the fingers as the trimming is performed to take advantage of all the angles this method affords for trimming. It may also be required to repeat the whole process several times until satisfied with the appearance.

It is important to trim this area short because it never receives brushing and will mat badly by the time the dog is next to be groomed.

Trimming the Kennel clip is done the same as the Puppy clip except there are no leg lines to consider since the legs are all clipped one even length with the blade. Anything not clipped to satisfaction would be considered a "high spot" along with the rest and trimmed as required.

Shaving and clipping the tail

A dog has two prominent terminal ends, the head and the tail. You see them coming and going. Because of this, any error would be readily noticed in these areas. Note that not all tails are alike. They may be long, short, docked or natural, bent, straight, recurved, screw twisted, erect, or drooped.

Poodle tails will usually be docked. A docked tail is one that has been surgically cut short between the vertebrae. This is done by a veterinarian when the dog is a week or two old. It may be done by a knowledgeable breeder as well. Docking is not a health measure, and is done for style appearance only. Some countries such as England prohibit docking as an inhumane act. In the USA, docking is a permissible practice.

A properly docked Poodle will have the tail shortened by allowing the tail to extend out behind the dog a distance of from two to four vertebrae. Unfortunately, on occasion you will find that the dog has been docked too close, with very little tail remaining. I have had occasion to create a false tail, by using the long hair above the anal area and shaping it to resemble a true tail.

Not all tails are set on the dog at exactly the same place. Some are set low, most are medium set, and some are set high. The high-set tails are the ones that will give novice groomers trouble unless the following instructions are strictly adhered to.

When shaving tails that have been docked, an A5-15 blade is used *with the grain.* Start by placing the back of the blade behind the rear right hip bone. Move the clipper to the left, making contact with the tail as you hold it in an encircling grasp with your left hand. The point of contact is the limit point of how far forward on the tail you may shave from. Do not exceed this limit point or a drastic error I refer to as "bull's-eye tail" will be created.

The tail will be shaved from the limit point toward the end of the tail a distance equal to one half the length of the tail bone. Shave *with the grain,* gradually shaving a small portion of one side, then the other side, then join them by shaving the top. When a small band is shaved, carry the line down further using this method until the halfway point is reached. Remember to shave half the length of the *tailbone,* not half the length of the whole tail, which would include the tassel or pompom as well.

When this portion is completed, change your left hand grip to the same one used when brushing or clipping Area 5. The left hand encircles the tail with the thumb pointing up. The underside of the tail is now exposed, and the dog must be made to cooperate and stand with the back legs well in position. Command "Stay," and shave *with the grain,* up, from just above the anus with the angle of the blade low, and use an extremely light flicking stroke on this most sensitive area. Too much pressure or too great a blade angle will abrade the delicate skin under the tail. This would cause a burning and itching sensation that would cause the dog to drag his rear on the floor, and constantly lick to try to relieve itself. It is poor grooming and should be guarded against.

A natural tail, one not docked, would not have half the tail bone shaved. Instead, an amount equal to that required to clear slightly past the anus would be shaved *with the grain*. Follow the same procedure for shaving as is done for docked tails.

Anal area shaving

Now that the longer hair of the underside of the tail has been removed, we can see better to shave the anal area. Note that the hair grows toward the opening of the anus from each side and from below it. Therefore, to shave *with the grain* it is necessary to shave with an A5-15 blade from both sides and from below the bottom of the anal opening. Never, ever, shave directly across the delicate mucous membrane of the anus. Always use a low angle on the blade. Always use short flicking touches of the blade, lightly, to avoid injury.

To accomplish this procedure, it is necessary to maintain absolute control over the dog to avoid the animal's sitting down suddenly and injuring itself on the clipper blade.

Position the animal "on station," front legs forward, hind legs fully extended. When a dog desires to sit, it must first move its hind legs forward to bend them, giving you advance warning and time to either reposition the dog or withdraw the clipper. Assuming from this point on that you are right-handed, you will now lift the tail straight up, vertical. Now place your left hand karate-chop fashion at the base of the tail with the little finger coming in contact with the spine at the tail base. Close your left hand firmly around the tail, and keep your left elbow down. In this position you should be able to deter the dog from sitting, and allow clear view and access to the anal area for shaving.

Remember, use short flicking light touches with the A5-15, and shave an area only as wide as the tail.

Trimming the tail

Not all tails are created equal, a simple fact of nature and man. Some are long, some are short. Some are sparse and some are dense. When trimming a Poodle's tail that has been docked, the following method, which I employed at Pennsylvania School of Dog Grooming, has proved safe, quick and attractive.

Grasp the tail in the left hand, palm up, and brush and comb *with the grain* to straighten all the hair. Measure by eye a distance from the shaved portion of the tail equal to two times the shaved portion toward the end of the tail hair. This will give you an idea as to where the tassel of the tail will be trimmed. Hold the tail tassel straight out with the left hand, your thumb just past the pre-measured length. With the right hand, working with your blunt tip scissor for safety, cut through the tassel immediately forward of your thumb. Now grasp the tail near its base and shake it. The tassel will now shake out to form a circle of hair that will be a semi-pom in shape. With the left hand, grasp the hair in the center of the tip end of the semi-pom. Holding this position, backcomb *against the grain* until the tassel resembles a miniature Christmas tree. Using your curved scissor with points turning in toward the dog, trim a small amount off the edge of the portion of the tassel closest to the dog. This will create a trim line, which will be trimmed all around the base of the semi-pom. Now move up slightly to the top edge of the trim line and trim it the same as the original edge. Continue the process until the "Christmas tree" has taken on a round ball shape. The size of the pompom you create will depend on how dense the tail is and how much is there to begin with. Dense tails produce the best pompoms, and return to their trimmed shape when the dog sits and then stands up.

It is wise not to trim very much when dealing with a sparse tail. There will be little body to hold it into position. Good dense tails on Poodles are scarce; unfortunately, most are so sparse that a good pom is hard to fashion and a pseudo-pom must be the type you must be satisfied with.

A tail that hasn't been docked, such as may be found on many a Cockapoo (Cocker Spaniel and Poodle cross breed), may be trimmed into a plume shape. This style eliminates the stringy, untidy look that this natural tail usually grows in.

The base of plume-style tails is either closely clipped or shaved just enough to clear the anus when the tail is in the down position.

Grasp the end of the tail tassel with the right thumb and index finger about 3⁄4″ past the end of the tail bone. Keep the tassel hair gathered in this grip. Now take the same grasp behind the right hand with the left thumb and index finger. Release the right hand grasp. With the blunt tip scissor, trim the tassel straight across immediately forward of the left thumb. Be sure your scissor is next to the thumb and not the finger or too much will be trimmed.

Pick up and hold the tail by the cut tip end and allow the balance of the hair to hang as you hold the tail out parallel to the table. This is important if the tail is to be trimmed to a pleasing length. Using the curved scissor with the blunt tips pointing toward the fall of the hair, trim a gradual curve from the previously trimmed hair at the end of the tail to the shaved or clipped tail bone. Recomb the tail *with the grain,* hold the end, let the tassel fall and retrim any stray wisps if required.

Tails on breeds such as Schnauzers and Cockers are usually docked, and are styled quite simply by clipping the tassel completely off to a blunt smooth finish. No scissor trimming is required.

The underbelly, groin, and genitals

Although the physiology of males and females, whose proper canine names are dogs and bitches, is not the same, the approach to this area is. The greatest difficulty for the novice will be to attain the proper control position. Also, the physical position the groomer must assume is awkward until mastered. I have never trained my students to stand the dog up on its hind legs while holding its forelegs so the dog is in a vertical position. This would allow for easy access to shave the belly, and a portion of the genitals. But problems are associated with this control position. Many dogs refuse to allow you to hold them in this position by their front paws, and your hands are in range of avenging teeth. Older dogs suffering with arthritis of the hind legs, and obese animals, cannot hold this position due to increased pain of the leg joints. In this standing position it is impossible to do a thorough job of shaving the groin on either side of the dog's testicles or the bitch's vulva. To accomplish this, the legs must be lifted to allow access. I have never had difficulty involving access, control, injury or irritation using the following methods for shaving the belly, groin, and genitals.

When working with a male (dog) canine, stand the dog on station and with the left hand grasp the right rear leg in an encircling grip just above the hock. Extend the left index finger straight out, pressing against the stifle joint. Lift the leg out to the side allowing it to bend, and then lift it up, but never higher than the spine supporting it at the stifle with the index finger. Do not pull straight back! You should now be able to see clearly under the animal, with the groin on the right side in full view. With the right hand, locate the umbilicus. On males, this will be about 1″-2″ forward of the penis. This is the point you will start shaving with an A5-15 blade. The hair on the underbelly grows just the reverse to that on the back, so you will start your shaving *against the grain.*

Shave the 1″-2″ section forward of the penis, then continue by shaving the belly beside the penis (not the penis itself). The penis will be shaved last. Shave to the rear until you arrive at the groin, that area where the leg meets the rear abdomen. At this point you must now shave toward the stifle joint, which will be *with the grain.* Shave the groin, the inside of the thigh to the inside of the stifle with light strokes, WITH ALL OF THE POINTS OF THE TEETH OF THE BLADE TOUCHING THE SKIN AT THE SAME TIME. KEEP THE BLADE SPRAYED COOL TO AVOID A CONTACT BURN. If all teeth touch at once, you will avoid injury due to the corners of the blade digging into delicate tissue. The testicles are shaved by making contact at the base of them where attached to the body, and then lightly shaving towards the table. This is *with the grain* only! The right side should now be complete with the exception of the penis.

The left side is done the same as the right, but with a bit more difficulty, due to position. Grasp the left hind leg with the left hand, same grip but allow the leg to pivot in your hand as you raise it out and up. Now place your left elbow on the table while holding

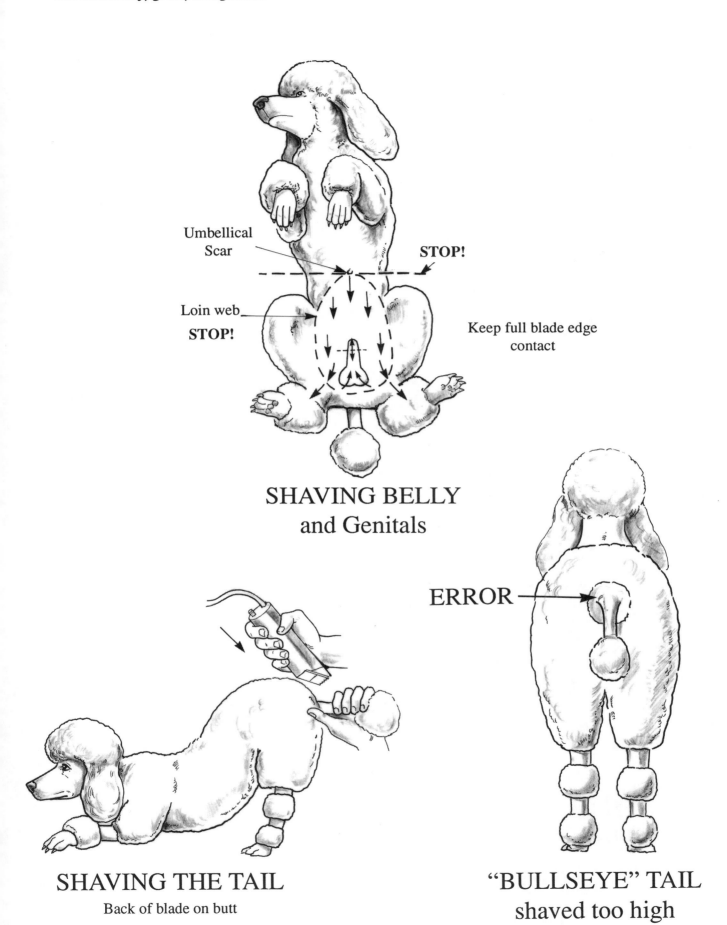

Umbellical Scar

STOP!

Loin web
STOP!

Keep full blade edge contact

SHAVING BELLY
and Genitals

ERROR

SHAVING THE TAIL
Back of blade on butt

"BULLSEYE" TAIL
shaved too high

the control position. You will find this a real help to hold the animal's weight in this position.

With an A5-15 blade in the clipper hand, cross your right hand over from right to over your left, and under the dog's belly. You will have to lean over to your left to obtain a good view of the area to be done. The control position is somewhat similar to clipping the left areas, numbers two and three. Repeat the shaving on the left side same as was done on the right, starting forward of the penis. When finished, it is time to shave the penis. Actually, you never do shave the penis because it is contained in a sheath to protect it. To avoid cutting the tip of the penis, you must slightly stretch the sheath toward the tip as you shave the area behind the fingers that are grasping it. Shave the tip end by stretching it forward of the penis inside, holding this position with your fingers as you shave *with the grain,* from the base to the tip. Never shave directly across the opening, rather approach it on an angle from both sides. Failure to do this this way could result in injury to the delicate membrane or to the penis itself.

To shave these areas on a female (bitch), simply do the vulva the same as the testicles on a dog. The absence of a penis makes the belly easier to shave. Simply start at the umbilicus (you can feel the scar) and continue down the middle without stopping until you reach the vulva. The controls are exactly the same for females as they are for males.

Although this procedure sounds confusing, I assure you, with practice it becomes relatively simple, safe, and efficient.

Trimming, clipping, and shaving the ears

The ears of Poodles, Lhasas, Cockers, etc., have tassels of hair that continue to grow. If not trimmed occasionally they become untidy and out of proportion to the overall appearance of the animal. When not properly brushed and combed, hair on the ears will mat and require removal by shaving partially, called "tasseling." Breeds such as Cocker Spaniels receive tasseling as part of their regular styling. This helps to prevent the matting condition that is prevalent in this breed. Some clients who recognize their own shortcomings may wish their long-eared pets other then Cockers to be tasseled or completely shaved off, in an attempt to prevent the matted condition. Tasseling of the ears is also valid when the dog has a chronic ear problem, such as mites, which may cause otitus. Foul odor, fierce itching, head shaking, and scratching are the result of ear infections. An ear heavily laden with hair will prevent air circulation, which will increase the warmth inside and production of parasites. Of course there are those pet owners who like the appearance of their pets when the ears are clipped or shaved off short. Some breeds such as the Schnauzer and Wire-haired Fox Terrier have this procedure done as part of the normal styling.

Matting, infection, and style are the prime reasons for tasseling or shaving.

By the time you have become proficient enough to work on the head of the animal, you are able to appreciate the controls required. The head areas are more critical work due to the proximity of the eyes, lip, and nose, and the loose floppy leather of the ears. The fact that the clipper sound is heard at so close a range when working on the ears causes some difficulty in execution of the procedure on some dogs. This is especially true to a greater degree when working on puppies for the first time. When you realize how loud it sounds to us when a fly buzzes past our ear you can easily understand why the dog reacts to the clipper sound, which is at least 100 times louder. And, of course, canine hearing is much keener than our own.

Before attempting to work the dog's ears you must discipline yourself to the controls required. If these are not learned and remembered, or are not practiced after being committed to memory, injury to the ear is almost a certainty. And in this area, injury can be extensive. If this sounds like a warning to you ... be assured that it is intended to be. To trim the length of the hair on full style ears, first brush and comb *with the grain* until the comb slides through without effort. The dog should be seated, as will be the case whenever working head procedures. Comb the ear down *with the grain* and then up also *with the grain* by holding the ear up between the first and second fingers of the left hand. Use the left thumb to keep a grasp on the ear by applying pressure on it as it slides through the fingers. Use the comb repeatedly to stroke through the hair in the up position until all the hair is extended upward. Now with the left hand slide the fingers upward to the edge leaving the amount you wish to trim off, grasp

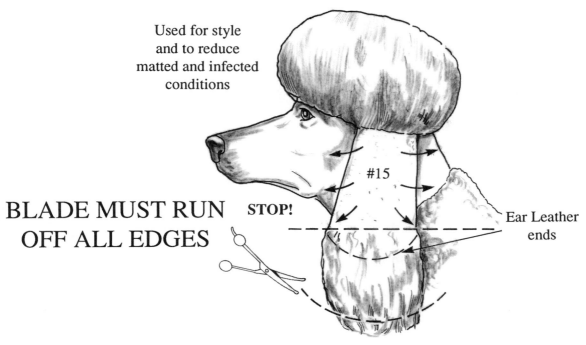

Used for style
and to reduce
matted and infected
conditions

#15

STOP!

Ear Leather
ends

BLADE MUST RUN
OFF ALL EDGES

TASSEL EARS

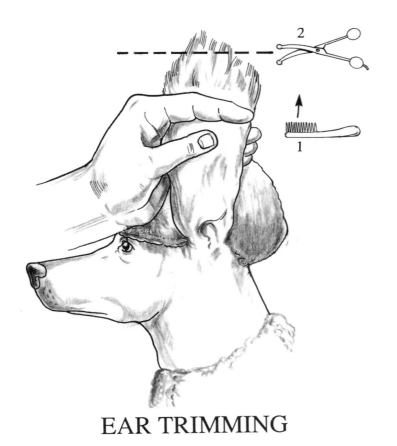

EAR TRIMMING

TRIMMING CORNERS
(Rocker bottom)

the ear with the thumb pressing it to the palm of the left hand, and lower the ear with the underside still facing you. With the dog in control, command "Stay" in a firm tone and, quickly with the curved blunt scissor, trim the exposed hair above the fingers. The tip of the scissor should be pointing to the edge. This way the curve of the scissor will initiate the "rocker bottom" shape that is desirable. Lower the ear and place it fanned out in the palm of the left hand. Holding the hair parallel to the table, trim the corners to form the rocker bottom edge of the ear. Now lower the ear all the way and check for wispy stray hairs and trim off. Repeat these steps on the other ear to complete this procedure. Tasseling the ears requires no brush and comb preparation, since the hair is going to be removed instead of preserved. Start by holding the ear in the palm of the left hand, outer side up. Control is established by seating the dog and commanding "stay." The left thumb presses the ear to the palm as the A5-15 blade is stroked over it in an across the grain direction, with all blade points leaving the ear edge at the same time. Never shave lengthwise along the ear's edge. The blade teeth can catch the edge, cutting it unmercifully. As the blade leaves the edge of the ear, press the fingers of the holding hand up to meet the blade. This will force the blade to shave that edge smooth and clean of hair. Move the fingers along the edge and shave until within ¾" of the tip of the ear on both edges.

Turn the ear over so you can see the inside of the ear leather and repeat the same steps on the inside edges, stroking off the edge across the grain as before. The remaining hair is the tassel. The tassel is then brushed and combed free of mats, and then trimmed the same as is done for full style ears. Repeat these steps on the other ear in the same order to complete this procedure.

If the tassel end is too badly matted or not desired, shave all the way off the end.

If the client desires the ears trimmed very short, puppy style, just trim the same way as full ears but trim next to the ear leather on the edges with the curved scissor. Caution: A scissor cut can be worse than one done with the clipper. Keep the dog under control!

When the fullness of puppy-style ears is still too great for the client's taste, a clipped puppy style will be appreciated. Clip the total ear working off the edges. Use an A5-5 blade if the hair has wave or curl in it and is coarse. Use an A5-8 if the hair is straight and/or soft and sparse. The steps and controls are the same as for tassel ears.

Cleaning the ears, plucking and swabbing

I have elaborated in other portions of this work on some of the reasons for chronic ear problems. Another source is due to an overaccumulation of hair growth in the ear canal. As the hair fills the outer ear canal, cerumen, a natural earwax, accumulates on it, providing food for foraging mites. They will set up housekeeping in the canal and create an unhealthy condition that will drive the animal near crazy with itching and pain. Left untreated, the dog's scratching can cause a break in the skin of the ear that will lead to a secondary infection. The area is prime with bacteria ready to do a number on the poor helpless animal. Many cry in pain when scratching and rubbing in an attempt to relieve themselves. The more they scratch, the worse the inflammation. At its worst, a radical surgery must be performed, which is highly disfiguring. The best answer is to prevent the onset of the problem by regular proper ear care.

The dog should be seated and facing you. Use the left hand to take an encircling grip over the open ear, grasping the ear and side of the head at the same time. The object is to maintain control and keep the ear leather back and the ear open.

Note, when looking at the underside of the ear leather, that there is hair not only inside the ear canal, but also growing on the ear leather surrounding it. This ear leather hair must be shaved off prior to plucking the hair from the canal, to avoid pulling it in the process, in which case the dog will wince in pain and refuse to allow you to continue with the procedure. Shave the area clean with an A5-15 blade, first cross grain around the canal opening, and then cross grain and *against the grain* on the leather portion that is lightly covered with hair. Do not shave out to the extreme edge of the ear as when tasseling. Normally, the pink-colored leather will dictate the area to be shaved.

Place a pinch of ear powder in the ear. This material is made to dry the hair inside and provide a good grip for extraction. Some powders also contain an antibiotic to fight the action of bacteria that may be present in the ear. Most contain a pine tree extract called rosin. This is the same material used on violin bow strings to produce vibration. Rosin is also used to produce a nonslip surface on the soles of prizefighters' shoes. I have found it excellent for providing a nonslip fingertip grip.

Still holding your left hand control grip, with the right hand, using a pinch grip with thumb and index finger, grasp a small amount of canal hair and twist and pull it steadily out of the canal. You will be surprised how easily it is extracted in most cases. The canal hair is not as firmly affixed as is the hair on the ear leather. Continue this steady twist-and-pull procedure until as much as possible can be accomplished with the fingers. To reach deeper into the ear canal requires the use of forceps.

PLUCKING EARS

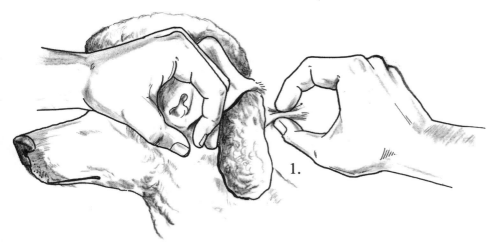

Fingers first

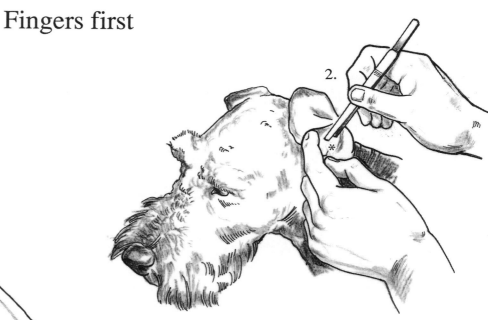

Dilate ear by
grasping lobe*, then
pluck with forceps and swab.

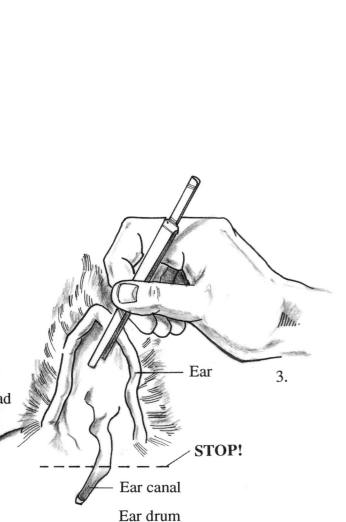

Ear

3.

ad

STOP!

Ear canal

Ear drum

Forceps for the grooming industry are available in two styles. Tissue forceps look much like long tweezers, with narrow smooth blunt ends. Inside the inner tip ends there are grooves that grip the hair tightly when squeezed. These are closed with the thumb and fingertips. Kelly forceps resemble scissors with a thumb and finger ring at both ends. These are larger than tissue forceps, and have a locking device on them that holds the forceps locked closed when engaged. Generally, I don't like to use Kelly's for normal ear cleaning. The grip is not as sensitive as with tissue forceps, and tender inner ear tissue is easily pinched and the skin torn.

To do a proper job with the forceps, the left hand control must be changed. Locate the hard cartilage that protects at the edge of the ear. This is the area that must be gripped with the thumb pointing inside the ear canal. A pinch grip is used. It's not much to hold on to, and several attempts may be required to get a grip good enough to work with. The left index finger may be used to hold the leather up and the ear open. In this case you would use your left middle finger and thumb to take the pinch grip.

The ear drum is located at the extreme end of the L-shaped canal. So long as you do not force the forceps, no harm will be done to it. You can insert the forceps down as far as you can see and pinch them closed on the hair with the right thumb and fingers. Use a slow steady pull to remove the hair. Do this repeatedly until all hair is extracted. Do not be discouraged if your first few attempts at dilating the ear are not successful. Once mastered, you will have learned a method known by a relatively select few, to do a perfect job in this important area.

Antiseptic swabbing

After all hair has been extracted from both ears, twirl a stretched out cotton ball around the tip end of the forceps as you pinch them closed on it. When twirled tightly it will stay on the forceps without pinching them, and you will have a large bud of cotton protecting the tip ends. This end is now saturated with 70% isopropyl alcohol. The ears are held the same as when using the forceps for hair extraction, and each ear is thoroughly swabbed clean of any wax and residue. Be sure to swab the shaved leathers as well. Change the swab as required.

Not only does this process clean the area, it also helps destroy mites, bacteria, and parasites such as fleas when coming in contact with them. Since alcohol is a dehydrant, it aids in the drying of any moisture that may remain in the canal. Naturally, ears that are obviously infected should not be serviced, but should be referred to the client's veterinarian for treatment.

Styling the face

The way the face is styled can affect the viewer's impression of the pet's demeanor. Leave the face covered with hair, neatly trimmed, and it looks "puppyish." Shave all the facial hair off, and some will say that the pet looks "snooty." A mustache imparts a more "formal" look, etc.

Nothing changes the appearance of a canine more than how the face and head are styled! The face and head is the part that is most looked at. It is the portion that is petted, hugged, scolded, and kissed the most. A wagging tail can be an indication of a happy dog. But I would never assume a dog's disposition without knowing what was going on on the other end. Is she snarling, showing her teeth, squinting with joy, wide-eyed or eyes lowered in fear or timidness? Some dogs smile — yes, actually effect a smile for attention — and others sulk when they are sad. None of these telltale signs can be determined by looking at the tail end. A well-groomed body may give the dog a beautiful appearance, but the styling of the face is what gives the dog its identity!

Facial styles can be basic and simple or more elaborate and complicated. All have one thing in common. The eyes, nose, lips, and ears are waiting targets for misguided clipper blades and scissors. As important as control and awareness is when doing other areas of the dog, it is doubly so when working the face. *Until you can hold absolute control over the dog, don't attempt to do the face!* This piece of advice and the reason for it should be obvious.

Faces can be styled straight or in variations of four basic styles. Listed in their most requested order over the past 25 years at Pennsylvania School of Dog Grooming, they are:

- **Monkey clip:** leaves the face hair covered except for the bridge of the nose and under the eyes.

- **Mustache and Goatee:** Permits hair to remain on the end of the muzzle slightly forward of the corner of the mouth, and on a regulated area on the lower jaw. The balance of the face is free of hair.

- Just a **mustache,** as described above, without the goatee.

- A **Clean Face** refers to one without any hair at all, and not to the dog's sanitary condition.

It should be realized that the facial style should be suitable for the overall style of the animal. The proportion of a mustache should be in keeping with the overall size of the dog. That which would suit a Toy would hardly be sizable enough for a Standard size Poodle. An oversized scissored mustache would appear out of place on a dog that was completely "cut down" Kennel style with an A5-7 blade. Naturally, the client's wishes should be respected, but you should make every effort to give guidance to decision-making that will reflect your professionalism. The end result will always be judged as your work. Your influence can make you look better as a pet care professional.

The instructions that follow are intended to act as a study reference, and not just an "as you do it" instruction sheet. You will be working in an area where the dog employs all its major senses. The way the dog responds to your commands and handling will determine whether you will succeed in accomplishing the procedure without mishap, if at all. You must be sure of yourself. Confidence is something the dog can sense, and yours will be reflected in proportion by the dog's cooperation. What this all means is that you must be able to carry out these procedures without hesitation, without stopping to check notes or other instruction sheets. This material should all be committed to memory. Once the facial area is started, a rhythm should be maintained until the total procedure is complete, for best control and safety.

Facial areas by the numbers

All facial styling will start by first shaving the bridge of the nose from inside corners of the eyes halfway toward the pad of the nose. The control grip is with the thumb under the lower jaw, and the balance of the fingers of the left hand spread firmly over the head just behind the eyes. Start with the dog seated, command "Stay" and shave with an A5-15 blade as directed, which is *against the grain.*

The Monkey Clip

This style leaves a hair covering over the whole face. This method is the least irritating to the skin of young pups and light-colored complexions. Older dogs appreciate this style since it requires no shaving of the cheeks or jaws, which are usually tender due to sore gums and bad teeth. The style also retains a more youthful look by simulating a puppy's face.

PROCEDURE 1: This is clipping on an imaginary line from the outside corner of the left eye to the top of the ear cartilage. This is the same ear portion that you hold when working with forceps.

The control grip is the same as the start position, except allow the index finger to wrap over the bridge of the nose just forward of the stop, with the thumb under the jaw.

With an A5-5 blade in the clipper and the dog seated facing you, turn the head a quarter turn to your left, fold the ear back over the head and hold it there. Clip cross grain, starting on the eye-ear cartilage line down to just past the lower jaw. Keep the points of the blade in contact with the skin to eliminate pulling the hair. Naturally, as is true with clipping on the body, the face should have been previously brushed and combed to prevent blade jam and snagging. If you snag the hair and pull it, the dog may not permit you to try again. Repeat the clipping of this area if required, and be sure to clip the area below the ear.

PROCEDURE 2: Holding the same control, clip *with the grain* over the exact same area, from the corner of the eye to the ear. Be sure not to clip higher than the imaginary eye-ear line.

PROCEDURE 3: Holding the same control, lower the clipper and, starting from the corner of the mouth on the same side, clip *with the grain* to the rear of the jaw, immediately below the ear.

PROCEDURES 4-6: Turn the dog's body so that the dog is facing to your right. Don't just turn the head — the control won't be the same. With your left hand, reach over the dog's back and then wrap your hand around the left side of its face with your thumb on the bridge and your fingers under the jaw. This is called a reverse grip. With the right hand, lift the right ear and place it behind and around the head, holding it with the left hand grip, or under the left wrist, if it is too short.

You should now have a clear view of the right side of the dog's face. The ear grasp will tighten the skin on that side for efficient, safe clipping.

Using the same method as before, locate the eye-to-ear imaginary line and clip the same as done on the dog's other side. Procedure 4 is eye-to-ear clip cross grain. Procedure 5 is eye-to-ear clip *with the grain*. Procedure 6 is from the corner of the mouth to the back of the jaw under the ear, clipping *with the grain.*

PROCEDURES 7 AND 8: Return the dog to a position with it seated facing you. Take a control grip with your left hand, thumb under the chin and the index finger over the stop. The other fingers are spread out over the head. Keep the index finger close to the stop at all times to avoid pressing on the soft spot just past the nose pad, which will shut off the dog's air. You now will clip two of the four quadrants of the lower jaw. Procedure 7 is the dog's left lower portion, on your right, and Procedure 8 is the dog's right lower portion, on your left. Your thumb should be placed nearer to the tip of the chin to obtain access to this area. With the dog's chin lifted, and nose held at a 45-degree angle to the table, clip *with the grain.*

PROCEDURES 9 AND 10: With the dog remaining in the same position, in the same control, lower the head for a few seconds. This will allow the dog to swallow. I'm sure you've experienced being in a dental chair having to swallow but not being able to during a prolonged dental procedure. I have always tried to show my client's pets more consideration by anticipating their needs. A comfortable pet is also more cooperative and easier to control.

Now place the head in the 45-degree tilted position again. This time your left thumb will be positioned on the lower portion of the lower jaw, covering the area previously clipped in Procedures 7 and 8. Clip 9 and 10 *with the grain,* from the tip of the chin close to the lips to 7 and 8.

Now shift your thumb up to the chin again and reclip the median line between 7-8 and 9-10 until there are no unclipped portions showing. A smooth clipped lower jaw should result. Move the thumb up and down as often as required to obtain it.

Monkey Clip Facial Style
Clipping Procedure
◆ Left Side ◆

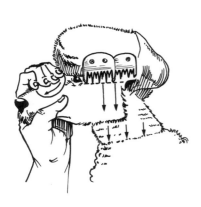

AREA 1.

LOWER AREA 1.

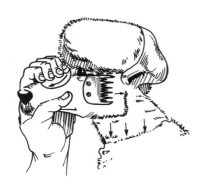

AREA 2.

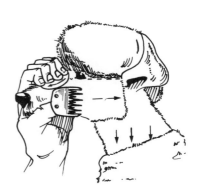

LOWER AREA 2.

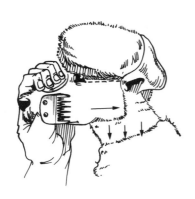

AREA 3.

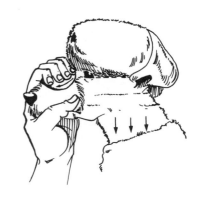

FINISHED LEFT SIDE

Monkey Clip Facial Style
Clipping Procedure
♦ Right Side ♦

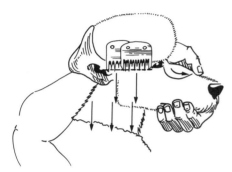

AREA 4.

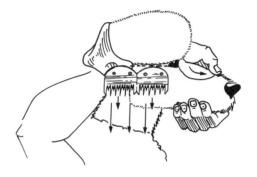

LOWER AREA 4.

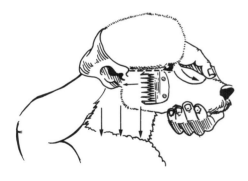

AREA 5.

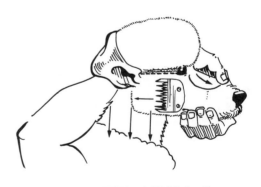

LOWER AREA 5.

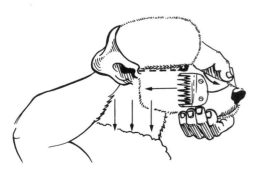

AREA 6.

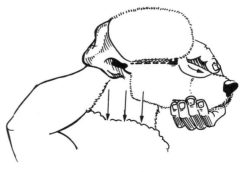

FINISHED RIGHT SIDE

Monkey Clip Facial Style
Clipping Procedure
♦ Lower Jaw ♦

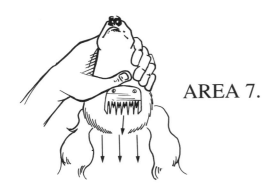

AREA 7.

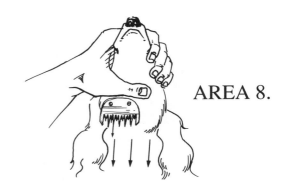

AREA 8.

AREA 7-8.
OVERLAP

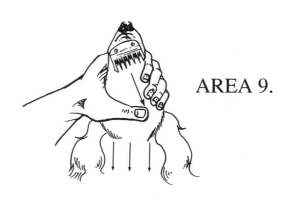

AREA 9.

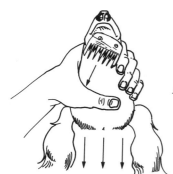

AREA 10.

AREA 9-10.
OVERLAP

Monkey Clip Facial Style
Clipping & Trim Procedure
♦ Top of Muzzle ♦

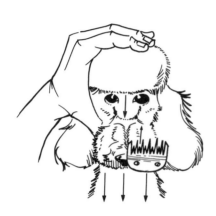

AREA 11.

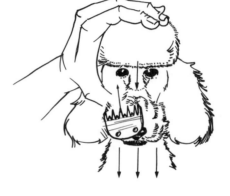

AREA 12.

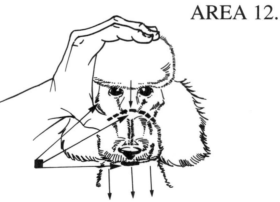

TRIM
SPOTS

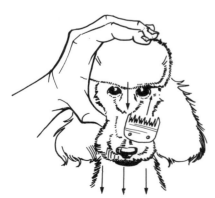

AREA 13.

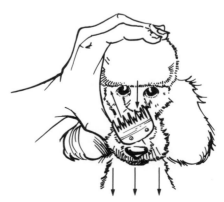

AREA 14.

PROCEDURES 11 AND 12: These are two quadrants of the upper jaw closest to the nose, located on the left and right and behind it. The same hand control is used as in the previous procedures, thumb under, index finger at the stop. The dog's head is held down parallel to the table the same as when the bridge was shaved at the start of this style. Clip *with the grain* over 11 and then 12. Note that a reverse grip is not necessary to clip 12 if held properly.

At this point, the total face should be clipped. Don't be concerned if it's not perfectly even. This is taken care of in the next procedure.

Trimming the Monkey clip

The angles and contours caused by the bony understructure of the face prevent the clipper from doing a perfectly smooth, even job. This is where the grooming scissor is employed.

Comb the face *against the grain* to lift all the unclipped portions up on the dog's left side. Sighting along the side of the face from front to back, trim away the uneven portions. Lift the ear and trim the large wad of unclipped hair just in front of it. Trim along the side of the mouth line with the mouth held closed.

Turn the dog to the right and, after taking a reverse grip, repeat the trim procedure on the dog's right side.

Reposition the dog to face you once again. Comb the hair on the bridge of the nose *with the grain,* toward the eyes, over the previously shaved area. Now scissor the overlap on the shaved portion only.

If all instructions were followed, you now have completed a Monkey clip face. When I first created this method of facial style, it reminded me of the cute face of a rhesus monkey, the type the old-time organ grinders would walk the streets with, to pick up pennies and tip their hats. The name stuck and the style has been one of my most popular facial clips, for reasons previously given at the beginning of this section.

Mustache and Goatee

Don't let the human application of this style fool you. The Mustache and Goatee may be used on dog and bitch alike, without discrimination. Not only is this a cute style for either sex, it also has a cosmetic use. Some canines are born with certain genetic defects that can spoil their appearance unless disguised. An astute pet stylist will display his or her professionalism by observing these defects and using justifiable reasoning to direct the client's choice of style.

Pets with an extended upper jaw will be termed "overshot." The upper teeth overlap the bottom teeth instead of being able to meet edge to edge. I've seen some overshot animals that were so severely deformed that the mouth was actually always open when viewed from below the jaw line.

The reverse condition, with the lower jaw extended, is termed "undershot." Although permissible and even sought after in some breeds, including English Bulldog, Lhasa Apso, and Pekingese, this is not a desirable feature in a Poodle.

The upper jaw and muzzle may be short and wide or long and narrow, which would be termed "snippy." The use of the Mustache and Goatee in combination, or separately when the situation directs, can overcome these visual objections to an otherwise beautiful pet.

A large mustache can hide an undershot bite. The overshot jaw can be corrected with a full Mustache and Goatee. A snippy muzzle can be made to look shorter and wider with a mustache trimmed or clipped to the desired width. Each style has its place, and should be employed when possible. Of course, a dog with a perfect bite may also be styled with Mustache and Goatee, or just a mustache strictly for style if that's what the client prefers.

The Mustache and Goatee is produced by shaving off all facial hair other than the hair on the end of the muzzle and chin forward of the corners of the mouth. Therefore, an A5-15 shaving blade will be used. The numbered procedures are the same as when doing a Monkey clip, but the direction in which the blade is used is reversed.

All facial styling will start by first shaving the bridge of the nose from the inside corners of the eyes halfway toward the pad of the nose. The control grip is with the thumb under the lower jaw, and the balance of the fingers of the left hand spread firmly over the head just behind the eyes. Start with the dog seated, command "Stay" and shave with an A5-15 blade as directed, which is *against the grain*.

PROCEDURE MG1: This is shaving on an imaginary line from the outside corner of the left eye to the top of the ear cartilage. This is the same ear portion that you hold when working with forceps.

The control grip is the same as the start position, except allow the index finger to wrap over the bridge of the nose just forward of the stop, with the thumb under the jaw.

With an A5-15 blade in the clipper and the dog seated facing you, turn the head a quarter turn to your left, fold the ear back over the head and hold it there. Shave cross grain starting on the eye-ear cartilage line down to just past the lower jaw. Keep the points of the blade in contact with the skin to eliminate pulling of the hair. The face need not have been previously brushed and combed to prevent blade jam or snagging, as was true when clipping the Monkey clip. A shaving blade will perform where a clipping blade will not. Usually one stroke cross grain is sufficient to "set the line." Be sure you have shaved close enough to the ear and below it.

PROCEDURE MG2: Holding the same control, shave *against the grain* over the exact same area, from the ear cartilage to the outside corner of the left eye. Be sure not to shave higher than the imaginary eye-ear line.

Mustache & Goatee
Shaving Procedure
◆ Left Side ◆

AREA 1.

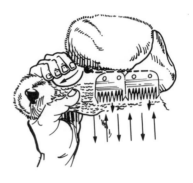

LOWER AREA 1.

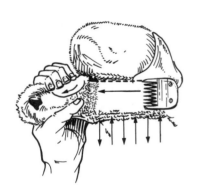

AREA 2.

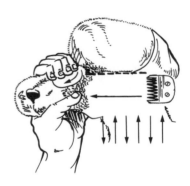

LOWER AREA 2.

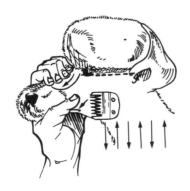

AREA 3.

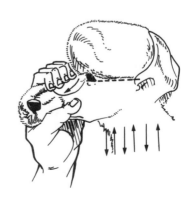

FINISHED LEFT SIDE

Mustache & Goatee
Shaving Procedure
◆ Right Side ◆

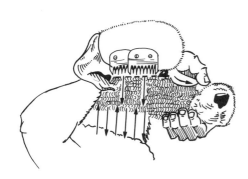

AREA 4.

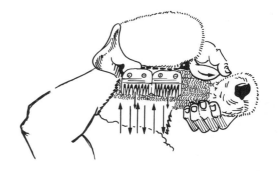

LOWER AREA 4.

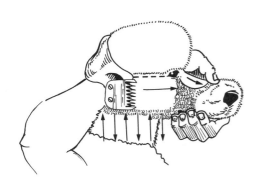

AREA 5.

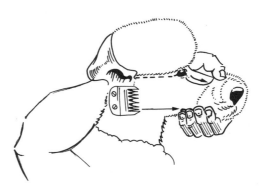

LOWER AREA 5.

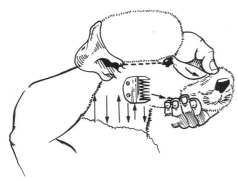

AREA 6.

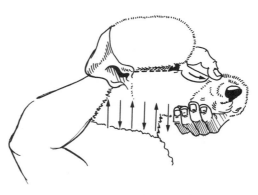

FINISHED RIGHT SIDE

Goatee
Shaving & Trim Procedure
♦ Under Jaw ♦

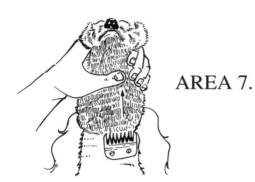 AREA 7.

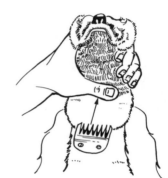 AREA 8.

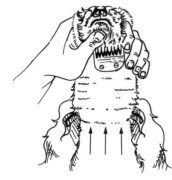 AREA 9-10.
OVERLAP–
SHAVE OFF

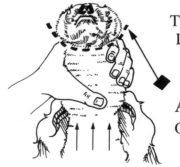 TRIM
LINE–
GOATEE

AREA 9-10.
OVERLAP–
SHAVE OFF
COMPLETED

Mustache
Shaving & Trim Procedure
♦ Top of Muzzle ♦

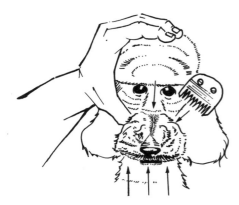

AREA 13.

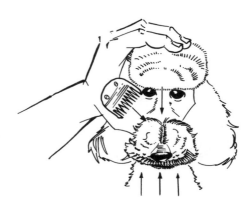

AREA 14.

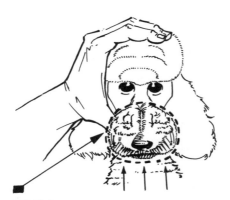

TRIM
LINE–MUSTACHE

PROCEDURE MG3: Holding the same control, lower the clipper and, starting from the area immediately below the previously shaved portion next to the ear, shave *against the grain,* **to** the corner of the mouth.

PROCEDURES MG4-MG6: Turn the dog's body so that the dog is facing to your right. Don't just turn the head — the control won't be the same. With your left hand, reach over the dog's back and then wrap your hand around the left side of its face with your thumb on the bridge and your fingers under the jaw. While holding this reverse grip, use your right hand to lift the right ear. Place it behind and around the head, holding it with the left hand grip, or under the left wrist if it is too short.

You should now have a clear view of the right side of the dog's face. The ear grasp will tighten the skin on that side for efficient, safe shaving.

Using the same method as before, locate the eye-to-ear imaginary line and shave the same as done on the dog's other side. Procedure MG4 is eye-to-ear shave cross grain. MG5 is ear-to-eye shave *against the grain.* MG6 is to hold the same control and, lowering the clipper and starting from the area immediately below the shaved portion next to the ear, shave *against the grain* **to** the corner of the mouth.

PROCEDURES MG7 AND MG8: Return the dog to a position with it seated facing you. Take a control grip with your left hand thumb under the chin, and the index finger over the stop. The other fingers are spread out over the head. Keep the index finger close to the stop at all times to avoid pressing on the soft spot just past the nose pad, which will shut off the dog's air. Now shave two of the four quadrants of the lower jaw. Procedure MG7 is the dog's left lower portion, on your right, and Procedure MG8 is the dog's right lower portion, on your left. Your thumb should be placed nearer to the tip of the chin to obtain access to MG7 and MG8. With the dog's chin lifted, and the nose held at a 45-degree angle to the table, shave MG7 on your right and then shave MG8 on your left, both *against the grain.*

PROCEDURES MG13 AND MG14: The dog will remain in the same position, in the same control, but with the muzzle held parallel to the table. The MG13 procedure is started from a point at the outside corner of the dog's left eye. Shave *against the grain* to the line established when the bridge of the nose and the side of the face were shaved. Rethink this area before proceeding. When shaved, only area MG11 will remain on the dog's left side. Take a reverse grip and shave the dog's right side portion of the muzzle, MG14, the same as you did on the left side. Area MG12 remains.

Styling the Mustache and Goatee

The hair that now remains on the forward portion of the muzzle and chin may now be fashioned into the Mustache and Goatee facial style. A short version of this style may be easily accomplished by clipping the remaining hair with an A5-4 or A5-5 blade. The amount of fullness desired would determine which is used.

Seat the dog facing you with the same control grip as used previously. Command "Stay" and run the blade *with the grain* starting just behind the nose on both sides, areas MG11 and MG12. Now lift the dog's chin up to a 45-degree angle. Be sure the mouth is held shut with no chance of the dog's sliding his tongue out and licking. Run the blade over areas MG9 and MG10 *with the grain*. The final result will be shorter if these areas are combed *against the grain* prior to clipping. After clipping, comb all areas *with the grain* and scissor-trim the back edge, at the shave line, all around the muzzle and chin. The facial style is now complete.

A much fuller Mustache and Goatee can be styled by scissoring rather than clipping. Using the same control grip, comb all hair *against the grain*. Insert the comb from the front side of the hair as if to comb *with the grain,* but instead lift up and out all the way around. With the left hand encircled around the muzzle, support the hair in this up and out position. Use the curved scissor with the concave side closest to the dog to trim an even line around to form the Mustache and Goatee. Trim until the Mustache and Goatee is neat and compact. You may wish to shape the goatee a bit larger, since the mustache will have to be trimmed to allow for eye clearance. A scissor-trimmed facial style is recommended for any client who likes a fuller-looking face.

The Beard Facial Style

Although more suited to the Poodle with a straighter facial hair, this style is the answer for those clients wishing an even fuller facial style. The style makes use of the straighter hairs' tendency to hang, rather than try to stand it up as is required in the mustache style. This style, then, is well suited for Poodle mixtures such as Schnoodles (Schnauzer-Poodle cross), Lhasapoo (Lhasa Apso-Poodle cross), and Cockapoo (Cocker Spaniel-Poodle cross).

These cross breeds usually carry the genes that produce straighter hanging facial hair. Their fuller facial bone structure also benefits by the appearance of a beard, giving it a more forward look. It should be noted that this style also increases the amount of effort required to keep it attractive. Beards have a way of getting food imbedded in them that is hard to deal with for the inexperienced owner.

Start the style with the dog seated and facing you. Use an A5-5, A5-8½, or A5-15 blade. The last will give a more dramatic effect, since the lines will be more defined. All blades will be used the same. Shave or clip the bridge of the nose and the sides of the bridge from the inside corners of the eyes halfway toward the pad of the nose. Use an A5-15 or A5-8½ blade *against the grain*. The control grip is with the left thumb under the lower jaw, and the rest of the fingers of the left hand spread firmly over the head just behind the eyes. Command "Stay" and shave or clip as directed.

PROCEDURE B1: This is shaving or clipping an imaginary line from the outside corner of the left eye to the top of the ear cartilage.

The control grip is the same as the start position, except allow the index finger to wrap over the bridge of the nose just forward of the stop, with the thumb under the jaw.

Facial Style
◆ Variation & Conversion ◆

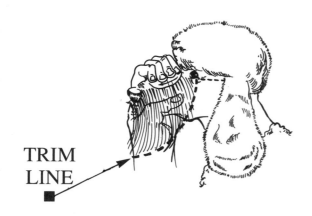

FULL BEARD
TRIM – DO NOT CLIP
AREAS 9-10-11-12-13-14

**TRIM
LINE**

MUSTACHE
SHAVE
AREAS 9. & 10.

CLEAN FACE
SHAVE
AREAS 11. & 12.

With the selected blade in the clipper and the dog facing you, turn the head a quarter turn to the left, fold the dog's left ear back over the head and hold it there. Shave or clip cross grain, starting on the eye-ear cartilage line down to just past the lower jaw. Keep the points of the blade in contact with the skin to eliminate pulling the hair, especially if an A5-8½ or A5-5 blade is being used. Be sure to brush and comb first to prevent blade snag and jamming.

Repeat the shave or clip procedure if required and be sure to shave or clip the area below the ear.

PROCEDURE B2: Holding the same control, shave or clip *with the grain* over the exact same area, from the corner of the eye to the ear. Be sure not to shave or clip higher than the imaginary eye-ear line.

PROCEDURE B3: Holding the same control, lower the clipper and, starting from an imaginary line dropped from the outer corner of the eye, shave or clip the area below the previously shaved or clipped area, *with the grain.*

PROCEDURES B4 AND B5: Turn the dog's body so that the dog is facing to your right. Don't just turn the head — the control won't be the same. With your left hand, reach over the dog's back and then wrap your hand around the left side of its face with your thumb on the bride and your fingers under the jaw. While holding this reverse grip, use your right hand to lift the right ear and place it behind and around the head, holding it with the left hand grip, or under the left wrist if it is too short.

You should now have a clear view of the right side of the dog's face. The ear grasp will tighten the skin on that side for efficient safe clipping and shaving.

Using the same method as before, locate the eye-to-ear imaginary line and shave or clip B4 cross grain. Procedure B5 is eye-to-ear shave or clip *with the grain.*

PROCEDURE B6: Lower the clipper and, starting from an imaginary line dropped from the outer corner of the eye, shave or clip below the previously shaved or clipped area *with the grain.*

PROCEDURES B7 AND B8: Return the dog to a position with it seated facing you. Take a control grip with your left thumb under the chin, and the index finger over the stop. The rest of the fingers are spread out over the head. Keep the index finger close to the stop to avoid shutting off the dog's air.

Lift the dog's chin at a 45-degree angle with the left hand control grip. Now locate a molelike growth that has a few whiskers sticking out of it on both the right and left side of the dog's face. These are approximately on a line drawn from the outer corners of the eyes under the chin to encircle it.

Procedure B7 is to shave or clip the hair on the dog's left lower jaw, below the whisker spot *with the grain* to the throat, and stop!

Holding the exact same control, turn the dog's head slightly to your right and complete Procedure B8 the same as you did for B7.

Now everything to the rear of B7 and B8 should have been shaved or clipped away, leaving only the hair which will be styled into the beard.

Trimming the beard

Numbers B9 through B14 will be part of this procedure.

The dog will be seated facing you and in the left-thumb-over-muzzle control grip. With a comb, part the hair of the beard from in front of the face, using the vertical line crease on the nose as a dividing line. Mother Nature has apparently provided the line for groomers to be guided by. Now, as you comb the dog's left side *with the grain,* hold the hair from the right side gathered under the jaw in the fingers of your left hand. This will prevent accidental incorrect cutting of this portion.

When the hair has all been combed down on the dog's left, use the blunt curved groomer scissors with the concave side facing the beard at 90 degrees to the edge to trim it. Start *at the front of the beard* at its longest point and trim from this point, a gradual curve that will end at the outside corner of the left eye. Maintain the control grip, recomb to check the line and retrim if not satisfied. Take a reverse grip, remembering to turn the dog facing to your right. Gather the trimmed portion of the beard in your left hand as you control the dog in your grip. Now repeat the trim procedure same as you did on the other side. You will have to turn the scissor so that the concave side of the curve faces the beard. Trim at 90 degrees to the edge from the longest point in front to the outside corner of the eye.

After both sides are trimmed and checked for stray wisps of hair, take a control grip with the fingers over the muzzle at the stop. Comb the beard down *with the grain* across the front of the mouth and chin. Now lightly trim a rocker bottom shape on the bottom edge, using the curved blunt scissor, the concave portion facing the edge at 90 degrees.

The final touch to complete the style is done with the clipper. Using the same blade that was used in procedures B1 through B8, shave or clip *with the grain* from behind the trim line at the point where the beard touches the skin, from behind the corner of the eye under the jaw to behind the opposite corner of the eye. The style is now completed.

Clean Face

This is the facial style always seen on Poodles entered in American Kennel Club shows. Because it is the most revealing of the styles, the dog should have the facial bone structure to carry it.

POODLE FACIAL STYLES

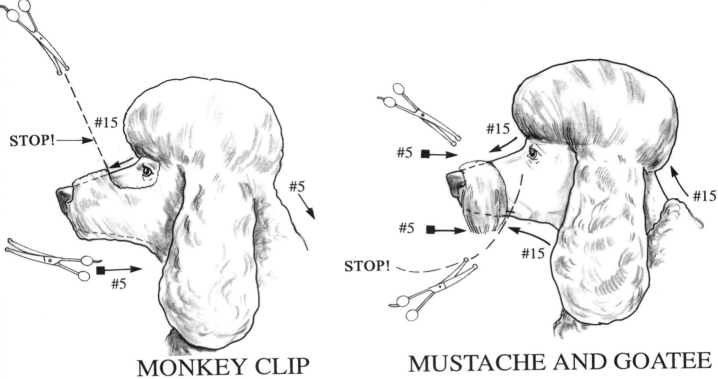

MONKEY CLIP

MUSTACHE AND GOATEE

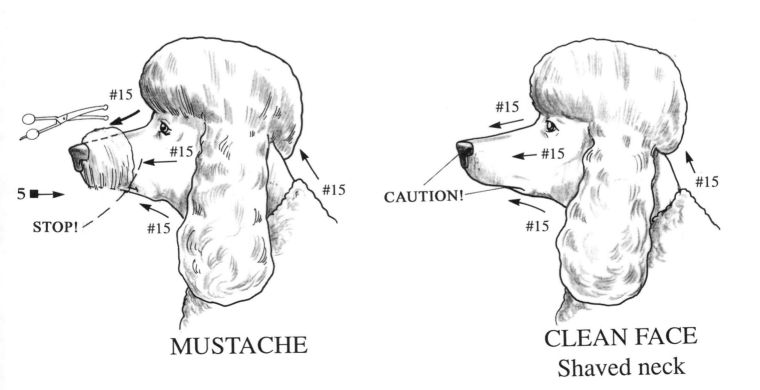

MUSTACHE

CLEAN FACE
Shaved neck

A very long narrow bone structure would look "snippy." An overshot jaw with buck teeth, or undershot with Bulldog-type teeth, would be unflattering on a Poodle, to say the least.

By shaving the face completely devoid of hair, these defects will be more obvious. The Clean Face style, however, does have certain benefits, and in some cases is a requirement without option. When dealing with ill-kept animals whose faces have become severely matted, a Clean Face will prevent undue discomfort and possible injury from excessive brushing and combing.

A clean-shaven face is also easier to keep clean on those dogs who like to submerge their muzzles in the evening gravy bowl. It is also a simple style to execute on puppies being groomed for the first time, though it may tend to be more irritating than the other styles due to the overall shave area involved.

If the puppy is very cooperative, and you hold good control, you may be able to complete the face clean with minimal potential of irritation. When well executed on a well-structured animal, a Clean Face can be a classy style.

Start the Clean Face facial style the same as if styling a Mustache and Goatee or Monkey clip. Shave the bridge of the nose from the inside corners of the eyes halfway toward the pad of the nose. The control grip is with the thumb under the lower jaw, and the rest of the fingers of the left hand spread firmly over the head, just behind the eyes. Start with the dog seated, command "Stay" and shave with an A5-15 blade as directed.

PROCEDURE C1: This is clipping on an imaginary line from the outside corner of the left eye to the top of the ear cartilage. This is the same ear portion that you hold when working with forceps.

The control grip is the same as the start position, except allow the index finger to wrap over the bridge of the nose just forward of the stop, with the thumb under the jaw.

With an A5-15 blade in the clipper and the dog seated facing you, turn the head a quarter turn to your left, fold the ear back over the head and hold it there. Shave cross grain starting on the eye-ear cartilage line down to just past the lower jaw. Keep the points of the blade in contact with the skin to eliminate pulling the hair. The face need not have been previously brushed and combed to prevent blade jam or snagging as was true when clipping the Monkey clip. A shaving blade will perform where a clipping blade will not. Usually one stroke cross grain is sufficient to "set" the line. Be sure you have shaved close enough to the ear and below it.

PROCEDURE C2: Holding the same control, shave *against the grain* over the exact same area, from the ear cartilage to the outside corner of the left eye. Be sure not to shave higher than the imaginary eye-ear line.

PROCEDURE C3: Holding the same control, lower the clipper and, starting from the area immediately below the previously shaved portion next to the ear, shave *against the grain* to the corner of the mouth.

PROCEDURES C4-C6: Turn the dog's body so that the dog is facing to your right. Don't just turn the head — the control won't be the same. With your left hand, reach over the dog's back and then wrap your hand around the left side of its face with your thumb on the bridge and your fingers under the jaw. While holding this reverse grip, use your right hand to lift the right ear. Place it behind and around the head, holding it with the left hand grip, or under the left wrist, if it is too short.

You should now have a clear view of the right side of the dog's face. The ear grasp will tighten the skin on that side for efficient, safe shaving.

Using the same method as before, locate the eye-to-ear imaginary line and shave the same as done on the dog's other side. Procedure C4 is eye-to-ear shave cross grain. Procedure C5 is ear-to-eye shave *against the grain*. Procedure C6 is to hold the same control lower the clipper and, starting from the area immediately below the shaved portion next to the ear, shave *against the grain* to the corner of the mouth.

PROCEDURES C7 AND C8: Return the dog to a position with it seated facing you. Take a control grip with your left thumb under the chin and the index finger over the stop. The balance of the fingers are spread out over the head. Keep the index finger close to the stop at all times to avoid pressing on the soft spot just past the nose pad, which will shut off the dog's air. Now shave two of the four quadrants of the lower jaw. Procedure C7 is the dog's left lower portion, on your right, and C8 is the dog's right lower portion, on your left. Your thumb should be placed nearer to the tip of the chin to obtain access to C7 and C8. With the dog's chin lifted, and nose held at a 45-degree angle to the table, shave C7 on your right and then shave C8 on your left, both areas *against the grain.*

PROCEDURES C9 AND C10: Remain in the same control position as before, with the dog seated and the chin lifted at 45 degrees. Shave *against the grain* over quadrant C9 by first sliding the thumb of the left control hand down to section C8. Follow up this procedure by shaving C10 using the same control, though it may be necessary to take a reverse grip to finish off the extreme end portion of area C10. This will depend on the length of the muzzle. Short ones will usually cause your own hand to be in the way when using the thumb under muzzle control grip. Whatever grip you use, keep the mouth closed to avoid tongue injury.

PROCEDURES C13 AND C14: The dog will remain in the same position, in the same control, but with the muzzle held parallel to the table. Procedure C13 is started from a point at the outside corner of the dog's left eye. Shave *against the grain* to the line established when the bridge of the nose and the side of the face were shaved. Rethink this area before proceeding. When shaved, only area C11 will remain on the dog's left side. Take a reverse grip and shave the dog's right side portion of the muzzle, C14, the same as you did on the left side. Area C12 remains.

PROCEDURES C11 AND C12: Keeping the same control grip as used for the previous procedures, lower the dog's head till it's parallel with the table. Shave *against the grain* area C11 on the dog's left muzzle end, and then area C12 on the dog's right muzzle end, using the same control.

As before, you may have to use a reverse grip for control for area C12. Be sure to keep the mouth shut to avoid injury to the pointed edges of the inner lips and tongue. These will cut and bleed if even just touched with the blade.

After the careful shaving of the last two areas, the Clean Face style is complete.

Through simple changes from grooming to grooming, a variety of different facial appearances may be had if desired.

Top skull styling

Believe it or not, a number of Poodle owners do not like the appearance of the usual Poodle style. Many will state, "I'd like my dog styled so that she doesn't look like a Poodle." In this case, you would do well to be sure that the client knows just what she is asking for before doing what the request would require.

The Poodle's coat and physical build lend themselves well to styling variety, other than the shaved patterns and facial styles usually associated with the breed. Good coarse coats on Poodles with shorter ear leathers can be styled similar to Wire-haired Terriers. This is especially true if the coat happens to be partly colored. A heavier body, short legs and long ear leathers would dictate a Spaniel-type style, if the coat is of the straighter variety. Medium-built proportioned straight-coated silvers with short ear leathers could be styled to resemble Schnauzers, etc.

Some owners will simply want their pet to look "natural," or so they say. Of course, the term natural can have a very broad meaning when used to describe a hair- or fur-growing animal that is usually groomed to prevent overgrowth and matting.

In most cases, I've found that a natural-looking dog request is best satisfied with an even-length clip all over the dog's anatomy. The exception to this would be a wider-looking leg to take away the skinny bent-leg shape associated with a Kennel clip. The finished clip would combine a Puppy-clipped body, a Monkey-clipped facial style, Terrier-style feet with the tops neatly trimmed to contour, ears trimmed fuller or shorter, a small tassel on the tail, and the top skull clipped to an even length rather than shaped into a pompom.

Simply put, think of all that usually comprises Poodle styling, and do the opposite!

Clipping procedure

Start with the dog seated, facing you with a conventional thumb over the muzzle control grip. Command "Stay."

PROCEDURE TSC1: With an A5-5 blade, or A5-4 if more fullness is desired, start clipping just behind the eye sockets toward the neck, which is *with the grain.* Your first strokes should be centered on the top skull. This will allow you to visualize the contour of the skull, while avoiding the upper corner areas of the ear, where they are attached to the head.

I cannot stress enough the care that must be taken to avoid the ear corners. The ear corner attachment is an inclined plane of tissue which can easily be caught between the teeth of the A5-5 blade. Severe injury will result as the blade tears the skin and penetrates the cartilage.

PROCEDURE TSC2: Fold the dog's left ear back and kink the ear leather so that it stays back by itself. From behind the left eye, clip *with the grain* toward the folded ear corner, and STOP at the corner.

PROCEDURE TSC3: Lower the left ear, and fold the right ear back and kink the ear leather so that it stays back by itself. From behind the right eye, clip *with the grain* toward the folded ear corner, and STOP at the corner.

PROCEDURE TSC4: Lower the right ear to normal position. Clip *with the grain* over the top skull behind the ears. Blend the clipper work into the neck area by using a scooping motion as the clipper blade leaves the back of the skull at the neckline.

PROCEDURES TSC5 AND TSC6: The top skull should be fully clipped at this point. The area where the top of the ear joins the skull will now need blending. With the ears down in natural position, clip across the grain from right to left on the dog's right ear to skull junction line. Be extra careful to avoid the edge of the ear, which can be caught by the blade and cut. Use the same scooping motion as used on the neck area to blend the anatomy.

PROCEDURE TSC7: With the dog seated facing you, control with the left hand, thumb under the chin, fingers spread over the head behind the eye sockets. Comb *against the grain* over the eyes to bring unclipped hair down over the eyes. Still holding the same control, using blunt-tipped scissors, trim away all the overhanging hair. Try to contour it to the shape of the frontal portion of the head. Trim so that no overhang remains, but to the same approximate length established with the blade used. Keep good control and command "Stay" before attempting to trim, to avoid poking the tip of the scissor into the eyes. If the dog refuses to stay, sometimes a slight shake of the head at the same time it is commanded will cause the dog to obey. Wait for the control to be established before attempting to scissor trim!

After trimming, recomb *with the grain* to check your work. The appearance should be a smooth, even transition from front at the stop to over the top skull to the neck. If not, reclip and retrim as required. When completed you will have taken the major step in styling the Poodle "so that it doesn't look like a Poodle."

Trimming the head pompom style

Although often referred to as the "topknot," this portion when styled for pet Poodles is not a knot!

A "topknot" head style would be accomplished by gathering the available hair, which should be abundant, and placing it in an elastic band or barrette. The long lengths that protrude out are then combed over the back of the dog and over and into the ears. This is the style seen on show-quality Poodles prepared for show.

The amount of effort it takes to maintain such a style makes it prohibitive for the average pet owner. It would require daily care to avoid matting and breakage of the ends of the topknot, which are usually oiled and wrapped in linen or plastic wrap, and banded.

The accepted practice is to trim a pompom, a semi-ball-shaped mass of hair, on the top skull. The final result of the trimming will vary with the texture, density, and physical structure of the hair. Harsh dense coats with an amount of bloom to them usually produce the best pompoms. One of the most difficult poms to shape are those "Poodles" who have been cross-bred with Spaniels, so called Cockapoos.

The hair can refuse to stand up when combed, and the pom takes on a natural part. The finished product often resembles a Roaring '20s human haircut.

PROCEDURE PP1: Start this procedure with the dog seated facing you. Take a thumb-over-the-muzzle grip and brush *with the grain* till smooth. Next, comb *with the grain* till snag-free. You will want the comb to be able to slide through with ease, before starting to trim.

The blunt-tipped curved scissor, with the tips pointing toward the dog, should be inserted into the hair next to the skull, halfway back on top of the ears at the point where they meet. The trimming should follow an imaginary line drawn from behind the ears to the opposite ear. The line will also fall behind the skull, where it meets the back of the neck.

The scissor work on this line should be six to eight well-spaced cuts in a curve from one ear to the other. The hair should then be combed *with the grain* over and through the previously cut area. This will set up a trim line, which will be at the position of the initial cut line. Angle the scissor slightly toward you and cut the top edge of the previous trim line. Recomb *with the grain* and repeat until the trim line is about even with the front of the ear leather. The amount taken off at the trim line should be about ¼" of each line. It could take you 40 or more cuts to get to this portion of the pom.

PROCEDURE PP2: Comb all hair *against the grain* forward, over the stop and eyes. Now trim off at the stop area holding the scissor at 90 degrees to the muzzle. The curve of the scissor should be the concave portion facing the dog, trim over the eyes curving

TRIMMING HEAD POMS

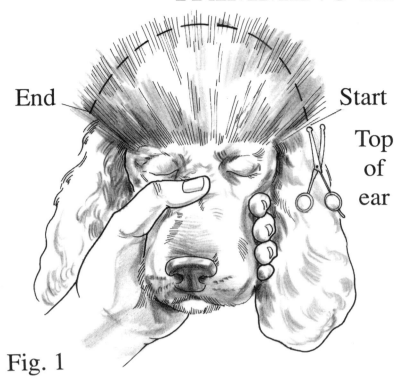

End   Start

Top
of
ear

Fig. 1

Trimming Poms
Top view of
back line

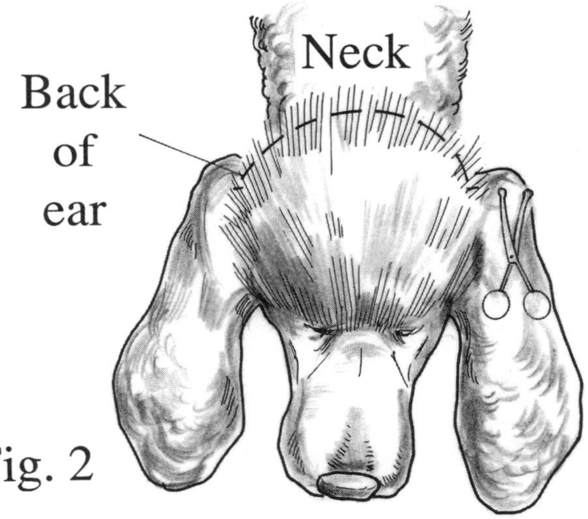

Neck

Back
of
ear

Fig. 2

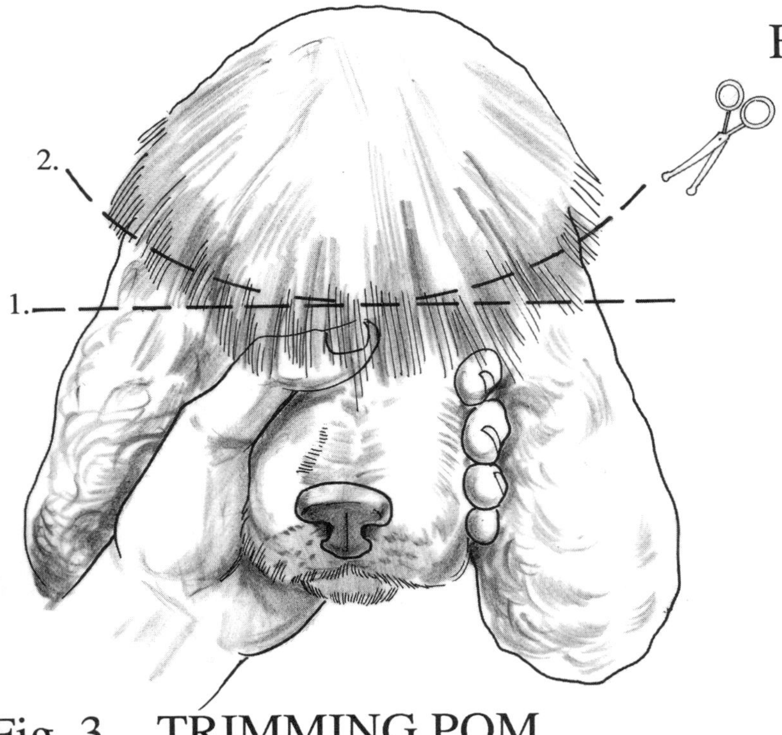

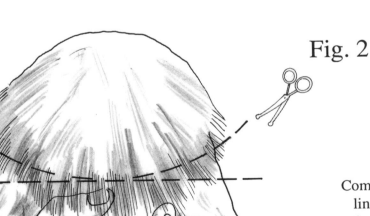

2.

1.

Comb forward. Trim from
line across stop corner
of eye to opposite corner
of eye. Cut is made
STRAIGHT UP – 90° to
dog's muzzel.

Fig. 3   TRIMMING POM

TRIMMING POMS
Hair parted to each side

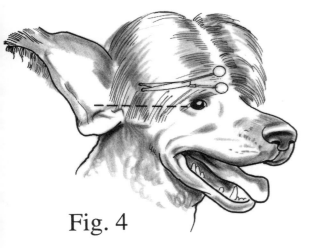

Fig. 4

SIDE TRIM LINE
Corner of eye to
top of cartlidge lobe
INSIDE of each ear.

COMB AND REPEAT
to desired contour

#3
#2
#1

LIFT UP STRAIGHT

First
cut
line

Second
cut
line

Fig. 5

"HORIZON" LINE
TRIMMING

CONTOURED
AND
COMPACT

Fig. 6

FINISHED POM

the scissor around to match the contour of the front of the skull. When done, comb and retrim the same area. You will find each time you comb that an amount of hair will be exposed that wasn't previously. The process must be repeated until you are satisfied that the front line is even and free of unruly stray wisps. Scissor cuts at this time could total 100.

PROCEDURE PP3: Part the hair in the center and comb cross grain to each side.

What you will now be looking for is the hair that may overhang the eye-ear line discussed in facial styles. Holding the scissor so that the blades are almost flat against the side of the line, trim off any excess at the line. Repeat on the opposite side and recomb to check progress. Repeat until accomplished.

PROCEDURE PP4: Comb all hair *with the grain* to the rear skull trim line and recheck the contour of the back portion of the pompom. If it looks smooth and shaped in transition to the top portion, leave it for now.

PROCEDURE PP5: Recomb all hair *against the grain* to the front of the skull again and recheck the front contour of the pompom. Make sure that there is no long straggly hair overhanging the eyes. The trim line should be neat and even.

PROCEDURE PP6: With the hair still forward, insert your comb just above the eyes and lift straight up. The hair should stand erect and look like a small fan when viewed from the front. As you hold the dog's muzzle, tilt the head up a little until you can see just over the top of the portion lifted. You will be able to note wispy lengths that no longer belong there. Try to view through them and sight the floor or the wall behind them. You will trim these wisps off until you achieve compact hair.

Do the following to promote a smooth "horizon line." Start with the blunt scissor, concave portion facing the dog. Trim with tip of scissor pointing up toward the ceiling on the dog's left side of the "horizon line." Trim right to left over the top of the developing pompom and down on the other side. The tip of the scissor will end up pointing to the floor when done correctly. By now you have probably taken 125 or more cuts if the lines are smooth.

Reinsert the comb and move the line up and back about ¾″ and trim as before. Continue until you arrive at the back of the top skull line where you first started the pom in PP1. Comb forward, *against the grain,* and use the comb to stand the hair up all over the top skull to evaluate your trim. Hold the muzzle in a skull grasp. You may now shake gently and the pompom will fall into place, as it will later when the dog runs. If the pompom "blossoms" out full and even, you are finished. If required, repeat PP6 until satisfied with the results. Note: It is not unusual to use as many as 150 scissor cuts to complete the total pom. Be patient!

Fancy styles and Poodle patterns

Probably more has been written about Poodle styling and "pattern setting" than has been about any other breed. This is because the number of styles or patterns that may be "set" on the breed is limited only to the groomer's own imagination.

The idea of pattern shaving, clipping, and scissoring came about more than a century ago as a necessity rather than as a beauty treatment. Standard Poodles, which were used much as a hunting retriever is today, were relieved of the coat covering the legs and hindquarters to allow for free swimming. The heavy coat that normally covers these areas would create drag in the water, and hamper the dog's ability to swim efficiently. Some areas of the chest and legs were allowed to remain covered with hair to protect the vital organs and joints from the cold water chill. Eventually, this remaining hair was trimmed into pleasing shapes to make the shaggy animal more attractive. From that humble start have evolved the unique and sometimes intricate patterns that are set on pet Poodles today.

Not to be confused with show dog patterns, which more closely resemble the original utility clips for hunting Poodles, pet patterns can be a wild and often shocking sight to see to those not accustomed to it. Today's styling extends past simple clipping and shaving to dying with colors and ornamentation with polish, rhinestones, artificial flowers, ribbon, beads, and sparkle dust. Shave patterns take the shape of corkscrews, Indian Mohawk and spike styles much the same as the human counterpart fads. Today's pet styling competitions allow a classification for creative styling, which encompasses all the above, and even decorative clothing to emphasize the style or mood that the groomer is attempting to project. These of course are the extremes.

Today's pet owner is more inclined to request a more natural-looking clip, in keeping with today's standards. More healthy diets, exercise, and conservation of natural resources also lead owners to look for a back-to-nature approach for their pets. However, a professional should have the knowledge required so as to be able to respond to owner questions, and be able to produce the look they may request, regardless of personal taste.

Many books have been published dealing with Poodle patterns of various types, so I won't waste space in repetition. However, unfortunately, too many of these so-called pattern books lack the precise detail required to accomplish the pattern the first time without error. It would appear that many are designed for those who already know how to pattern Poodles, and are intended to advance their knowledge of the process with a greater variety of styles presented. Of course, these are also intended to be used on the ideal dog for the style, which in itself can be a confusing task for the inexperienced. For example, to style leg pompoms on a pet whose size is dwarfed by very short stumpy legs would be to call attention to the fact unnecessarily. Instead of adding to the appearance, it would detract and make the pet look foolish. Therefore, the following is intended for those who may desire to set patterns, and will be doing

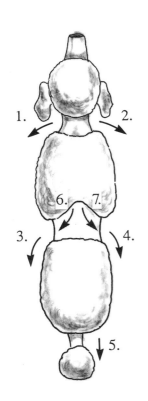

VANITY CLIP
pattern with
#15

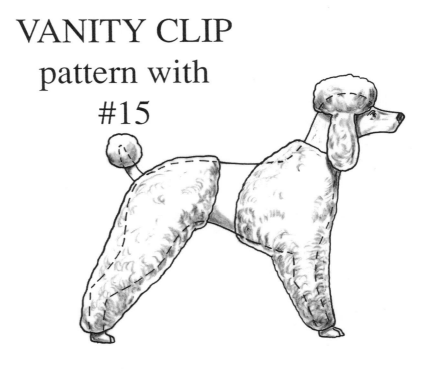

BOLERO DUTCH
pattern with
#15 and #8/8

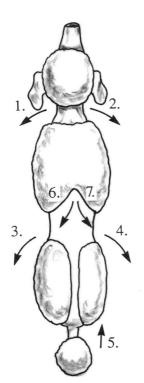

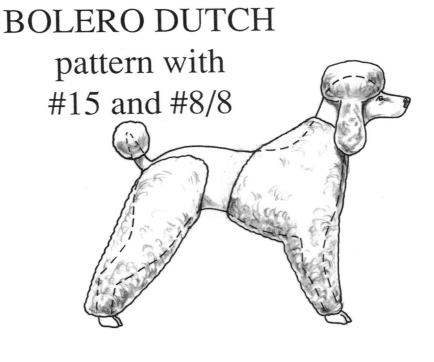

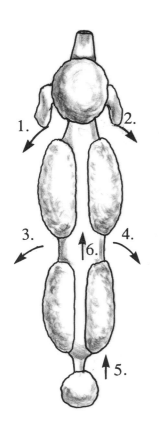

ROYAL DUTCH
pattern with
#15 and #8/8

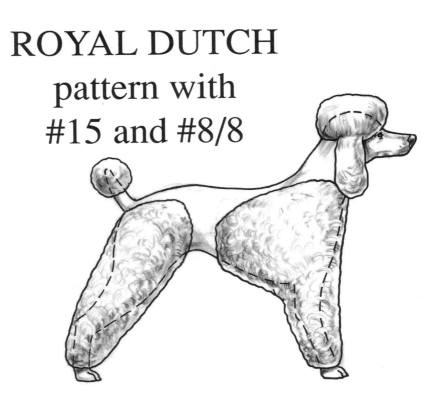

TOWN AND COUNTRY
pattern with
#15 and #8/8

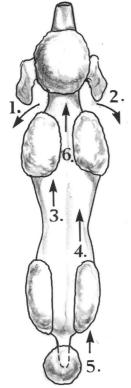

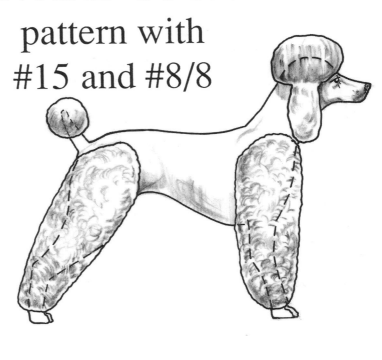

it for the first time. This is also intended for those who may need more efficient control methods than they have been employing to attain the needed style in a minimum amount of time, with small chance of error. Once mastered, these basic patterns may be combined, or altered by adding or subtraction, and new more daring patterns may be evolved with confidence. All patterns may be set regardless of the body coat length; however, patterns do look best on full scissor-trimmed coats.

A few words of caution. Set patterns are accomplished by removal of hair or fur at specific places, to effect a gross change of appearance. If not done as specified, it can produce gross errors as well.

Set pattern: Wedding Band (also known as Pants and Jacket)

This is the simplest of all patterns. Start with the dog standing so that you are facing either side. Command "Stay," place your free hand under its belly for control, and start shaving with an A5-15 blade at a point behind the last rib from the spine down cross grain to the underbelly. Do not shave over any part of the loin web tenders or you will spoil the intended appearance of the patterns.

Reverse your position to face the other side. Place your free hand under the belly, command "Stay," and shave down cross grain from the spine to the underbelly as before.

Take a position at the rear of the standing dog and control by grasping the skin behind the shaved portion on the back.

Command "Stay" and shave *against the grain* to clean out the line previously established. As you proceed to the sides of the band, control by placing the free hand between the hind legs from the rear and, taking a handshake position, grasp the dog's right rear leg high up around the thigh. Use your index finger like pulling a trigger to draw the loin web skin tight. Now shave *against the grain* from the back of the line to the front to clean that portion of the band.

Repeat the procedure on the other side by taking a control position from outside the rear left leg, use your index finger to tighten the skin, and shave with A5-15 *against the grain* to clean the band.

To finish the pattern, brush both sides of the line towards the shaved area and scissor trim the hair that overhangs the pattern. Your Wedding Band set pattern is now complete.

This pattern is particularly good for dogs with long bodies as a cosmetic style to cause them to appear shorter. Visually the line breaks the body length by division.

Set pattern: Vanity

Start by setting a Wedding Band, using the directions for shaving and control as above.

Stand at the rear of the standing dog and place the A5-15 blade above the forward edge of the band so that the blade teeth are vertical to the spine, the same as when you set the first cross grain line for the Wedding Band pattern.

Pivot the blade so that the teeth face the shave line at a 45-degree angle, one half of an upside-down V. In this position, control by keeping the free hand under the groin from the rear between both legs.

Shave toward the wedding band shave line *with the grain,* holding the 45-degree angle as you set the line. Repeat the same procedure on the other side of the spine, completing the upside-down V pattern.

Keeping the same control position as before, shave *against the grain* to clean up the total shave area. The inverted V shape should make a smooth transition with corners rounded into the band area so as to become an integral part of it, not just a notch sitting on top of the shaved band.

Brush all hair towards the shave area and trim the overhang to a sharp even line.

Set pattern: Bolero

Begin this pattern by setting a Vanity style on the dog. Control by standing at the rear of the animal, holding a standing position. The free hand is placed between the rear legs supporting the dog with the palm up under the groin. Using an A5-8/8 or A5-7/8 blade, shave from the base of the tail *against the grain* to the Wedding Band line.

Since the line just shaved was done *against the grain,* no cleanup run is required. Stand at the right side of the dog, and control with the free hand placed under the belly, palm up, supporting the animal.

Using the same blade (8/8 or 7/8) *against the grain,* round off the corner formed where the previous shave line meets the Wedding Band line originally set. The radius of the corner should be equal to the width of the blade being used.

Repeat the procedure on the opposite side using the same control and blade as previous. Now brush hair towards the shaved area and trim the overhang to a sharp even line to match the balance of the pattern.

Set pattern: Royal Dutch

The Dutch boy pattern originally was based upon the legs of the dog being trimmed into pantaloons, such as a young boy in Holland would wear. These pants are also known as knickers here in the USA. The effect is achieved by trimming the legs to whatever degree of fullness is desired and trimming the bottom line above the shaved foot rocker-bottomed.

Regardless of how the legs are trimmed or clipped, the shave pattern is set the same. For simplification, it is described here as a continuation of the Bolero style.

Start by setting a Bolero pattern on the dog and then turn the dog around so that you are positioned with the dog facing you. Command "Sit" and "Stay." With an A5-15 blade, shave a neck line and throat line, starting behind the ears *with the grain*. The line shaved is to be equal to one half the width of the blade on Toy-size Poodles, the full width of the blade on Miniatures, and one and a half to two widths of the blade on Standards. Dogs with longer or shorter necks can be sized to suit the anatomy.

After setting the line *with the grain* using the back of the ears as a starting reference, shave the same area *against the grain* to clean up. It is necessary to repeat the process several times on the throat area where the grain changes on either side of the center line.

When the neck-throat line has been set, stand the dog up on all four feet, still facing you. Change your blade to an 8/8 or 7/8 as before and control the dog by taking a thumb over the muzzle, fingers under the jaw grip.

The dog's head and neck are bent down towards the table to stretch the skin on the back of the neck. Take a hammer-hold grip on your clipper so that the teeth of the blade are facing you with the blade end closest to the table. Command "Stay." From the apex of the V in the Bolero pattern, run a line *against the grain* by pulling the clipper toward you, over the spine, across the withers, to the shaved neck line. Maintain a steady even pressure with the blade angled at about 30 degrees, making point contact all the way. This line must be accomplished in one sweep of the clipper in order to stay straight and even in its width.

With the dog in the same control position, pull the clipper *against the grain* to round the corners that are formed by the spine line where it joins the neck line.

Brush all hair over the shave areas and trim the lines sharp and even.

Set pattern: Town and Country

An elegant-looking pattern, especially on dogs having long, well-formed legs and harsh coats. The Town and Country style is simply an extension of the Royal Dutch pattern, and as such is easily performed.

Complete the Royal Dutch pattern and then stand to one side of the dog with it standing on all four feet. Command "Stay." Use side standing control as before. With an A5-15 blade, shave cross grain from well behind the withers and shoulders to the under chest-belly area. Repeat the procedure shaving successive lines until you reach the original Wedding Band line.

Repeat the procedure on the opposite side of the dog and then, shaving *against the grain,* complete the body shaving portion of the pattern. You will have increased the Wedding Band portion of the pattern by three to four times its original width, causing the legs front and back to be emphasized.

All corners are now rounded as previously done, and lines trimmed by brushing over the shaved lines and scissoring the overhang to a neat compact appearance. Due to the great amount of bare area generated by this style, some owners may wish that an A5-7 or A5-8½ blade be used instead of the A5-15, especially in cold climate areas. The blade used may also be altered based upon the texture of the coat and the youth of the animal to avoid irritating sensitive skins with too close a shave or clip. In these cases, use the desired blade *with the grain.*

Set pattern: Beachcomber

As with all patterns, any blade may be used to establish the fullness of the pattern. The Beachcomber is a summer clip and as such should have the body work clipped fairly close. For dogs who are mostly house pets that wear coats, sweaters, and even boots and leggings in the winter, the body length doesn't have to be dictated by the weather, the style being the deciding factor as to what blade would produce the best-looking pattern. Generally, the beachcomber is done with an A5-7 or A5-8½ blade and does a good job of delineating the areas that are to be trimmed into pompoms on the legs.

Start by clipping the entire body as usually done, with an A5-7 or A5-8½ blade, *with the grain.* Clip the hind legs to within one inch over the top of the hocks. Clip the front legs an amount above the second joint, equal to the amount left below it, afer the feet are styled!

This pattern looks best with Poodle-style shaved feet. Finish the feet, whatever style prior to the trimming procedure!

The dog should be bathed prior to trimming the pompoms around the legs to effect a better bloom on the coat and better trim to the pom. If a Clippin' Sling™ is used for the foot shaving operation, the trimming of the pompoms may be done after that procedure. The greatest control possible is gotten by having the dog suspended in the sling, with all four feet hanging in the air for easy access for shaving, trimming nails, polishing, and scissor trimming. From small puppies to arthritic geriatrics, a PSDG Clippin' Sling™ has always been employed for these procedures at the Pennsylvania School of Dog Grooming.

BEACH COMBER
or
SUMMER CLIP

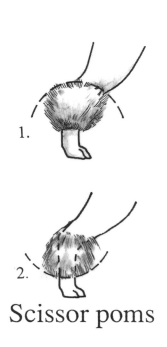

Scissor poms

PANTS AND JACKET
pattern with #15

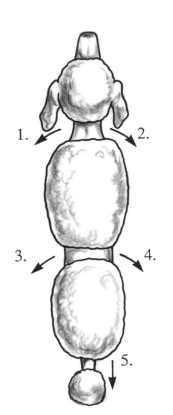

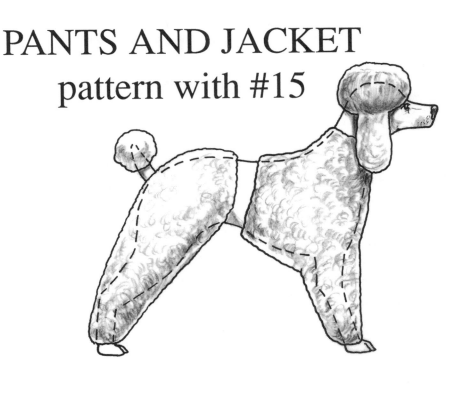

The hair remaining around the lower legs after clipping and foot shaving is then brushed and combed out thoroughly. Comb all the hair down *with the grain* over the foot shave line and trim an even line around the leg. Next, hold the scissor at a 45-degree angle to the edge of the hairline just trimmed and retrim the corner off all around the leg.

Comb the hair up *against the grain* and repeat the process. On the back legs, the top of the pompom line must finish above the top of the hock bone, with no exposure of it.

When the angle line has been trimmed all around both bottom and top lines, shake the leg to cause the hair to flare out and expose those areas that need fine trimming. Be sure to work all around the leg, circling it to make it a concentric compact ball shape. If your dog is suspended in a PSDG Clippin' Sling™, you will find it easy to work all sides by simply walking around it. If working the pompoms on the table, it will be necessary to hold each leg up in position as you trim, working one half trimming it and then the other. When trimming the front legs, it will help to flex them back at the second joint occasionally to observe the ball shape forming.

Remember to trim to size first before attempting to fine-trim. Also, be sure to match the size of each pair of poms to each other. Don't be alarmed if the rear pompoms are kind of upside-down pear-shaped. Unless you have a large amount of hair present prior to the start of the hind leg poms, the shape will be slightly tapered toward the bottom due to the shape of the hock bone. Continue to comb, shake and trim until you're satisfied with the outcome. Work patiently, as it may take as many as 75 individual scissor cuts to complete just one pompom.

This style definitely looks best on well-proportioned animals with great quality and texture to the coat to hold the pom's shape.

Pompoms added to set patterns

Any set pattern may have pompoms added to it if desired, so long as the dog's overall build will carry them. Poms may be added to all four legs or to just the front ones. Although it could be done, I wouldn't suggest adding poms to just the back legs. Doing so gives the appearance of a mistake or an unfinished job.

Pompoms are added by clipping with an A5-7 or A5-8½, or shaving with an A5-15 blade *with the grain*.

To add front poms, clip or shave the entire front legs, starting just below the elbow to an amount above the second joint of the leg equal to the same amount being left below it. This will be greater on a Miniature and less on a Toy. Finish the trimming of the poms the same as for a Beachcomber pattern.

To add rear poms, clip or shave a narrow band on the rear legs, starting one inch above the hock bone. For Standard size Poodles, make the band three inches, for Miniatures two inches, and for Toys one inch. This will provide the separation required to enable you to trim the balance of the lower legs into poms, same as the Beachcomber pattern.

Altering set pattern varieties

By altering the fullness of the coat through blade changes or by scissor trimming, a pattern can take on a fresh appearance. Before going to a complete change in pattern, it may be better to change the fullness previously employed. When a pattern change is desired, try to make the transition to the next closest pattern to the previous. A Wedding Band pattern can be altered to a Royal Dutch easier than the reverse, unless a longer than usual amount of time between groomings is allowed. The same would hold true in attempting to alter a Beachcomber to a Town and Country pattern.

One last word of advice regarding set patterns. Be sure the owner fully understands what they may be requesting, or what you are suggesting. Use pictures of the pattern if required. I had many a client request that their pet's "legs be shaved," when what they really wanted was shaved feet. What a drastic irreversible mistake if taken at their word!

SETTING BOWS

Fig 1.
START POSITION

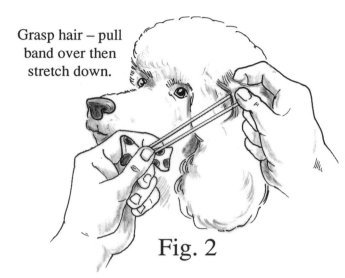

Grasp hair – pull band over then stretch down.

Fig. 2

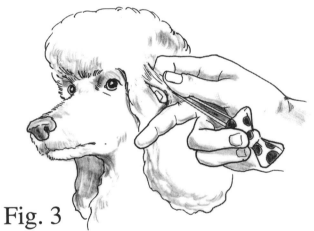

Fig. 3

Stretch – Hold position

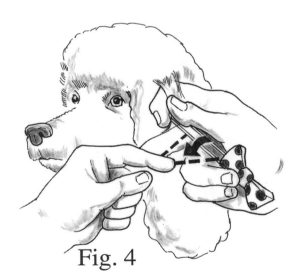

Fig. 5

Band pull over

Fig. 4

Pull band over left index finger (See Fig. 5)

ig. 6

Band Twist –
Note cross over
and two fingers
inserted prior to
twist

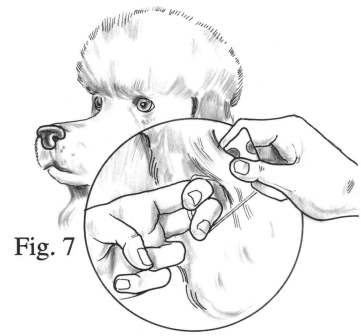

Fig. 7

Hair pushed through
twisted band – bow
pulled up

Fig. 8

Completed set bow

Finished fancy
look – bows

Avoiding personal injury: eleven key points

In any profession or trade that involves the use of hand or machine tools, there is a constant element of risk of injury. The surgeon doctor may be cut and infected if careless with his scalpel and needle sharps. A carpenter often will be cut with saws or injured with a hammer blow. Even office workers are subject to accidental paper cuts while filing.

In the dog grooming business we have the usual risks of tool injury, since we use sharp blades and scissors. We additionally have a greater unpredictable risk of being injured, not by accident, but intentionally by an animal bite. Knowing how to avoid or lessen the potential of injury and infection is important to the success and well-being of any groomer. Unfortunately, many subject themselves to injury possibilities or work in fear needlessly due to never having been taught otherwise. Other reasons are laziness, forgetfulness, and not working defensively.

Having worked with animals for more than 25 years, I have suffered nothing more than a Band-Aid type injury on only four occasions. I know that my safety record is no accident.

So what is the secret? It is simple: Develop a safe working habit, and stick to it! The safe working habit I have developed incorporates all of the procedures that follow. As you gain experience working with dogs you may add some that I may not have thought of.

1. Know the dog's name and use it before even touching the animal.

The dog's name used in a friendly tone can be the most beautiful sound you can produce for any pet. It implies that you know the animal, even if it doesn't know you. By calling the name first, you will get opportunities to contact and relate to the animal you won't get otherwise. Use the dog's name to preface a command. The name gets its attention so it can be attentive to the command. It lets the animal know you are addressing it specifically. In a crowded shop situation this becomes a necessity for absolute control. "Heidi, stay!" "Fifi, sit!" Be sure you don't reverse the order by calling the name last, or you will lose its purpose.

2. Be sure you can see the dog's eyes before making initial contact.

If you can't see its eyes, it can't see you. Your contact may become a frightening situation, and induce the dog to withdraw or, worse yet, bite. Put yourself in the animal's position. If I were to walk behind you, and touch you on your back without your being able to see me you would also be startled, or frightened. So it is with the animal. Eye-to-eye contact becomes even more necessary when retrieving a dog from a confined area such as a cage or kennel. Since the dog can't exit anyway except in your direction, it must do so willingly or it will retire to the rear and cower there, usually facing away from you. Until you can get the dog to face you and determine your intention, it may be unsafe to attempt hand contact. Calling the pet by name several times in a friendly tone may be just the trick needed to cause him to face you. Do this even before opening the cage door, to play it safe.

3. Make your initial contact with your hand clenched into a fist.

It's amazing how most of the public thinks it's necessary for a dog to smell their palm to become acquainted. A dog's sense of smell is so keen that he knows what you smell like before you are within ten feet of him, unless the wind is blowing in the opposite direction (not a usual thing in a shop situation). They will pick up the owner's scent several rooms away if each is served by a common heat or air conditioning system.

Protect those precious sensitive fingertips — don't offer them to a strange unknown dog to chew on. Make your initial contact with a closed fist, fingertips well protected by being tucked in. A bite attempt at open fingers usually will end up with a severe tear as you attempt to pull away from the painful nerve ending injury. A strike at a closed fist will usually glance off due to the size and lack of extending fingers to hold on to and penetrate. Too, if you offer little in the way of a target you'll be less likely to be assaulted.

After you've made contact with your closed hand, smooth it over the dog's back and chest, the area of accepted friendly contact. If you encounter no objection or resistance, it is safe to assume none will be forthcoming. Open your hand, pet the dog, and take physical control of it.

It is important, and I can't emphasis enough that all during this procedure, the dog's name should be used freely and in a friendly tone, along with whatever praise you might wish to use. It provides a distraction that allows you to make contact safely. It's another safe working habit that is worth developing.

4. Keep a choker-type leash on new or aggressive animals.

After the dog's own collar and leash are removed, immediately replace them with a choker chain or the new type plastic choker leash, prior to caging. Allow the free end of the leash to hang out of the cage.

Many dogs will go through a personality change when they are confined in a cage, crate, or kennel. Having only one point of exit, with you standing in front of it, will cause some to turn aggressive. They'll cower toward the rear of the cage, and fiercely attack if you attempt to remove them.

If you've taken advance precaution by placing a choker on them, you can extract a potential problem animal safely, with less traumatic outcome. Simply grasp the end of the choker, call the dog's name, open the cage door and tug gently on the leash.

Removing the dog's potential to resist or retaliate usually is all that's required to get him to submit. Once out of the confined area, they usually react the same as any other well-behaved pet.

Don't get complacent with a dog that has proved a problem and put him back in the cage without the choker. If they react once, they'll do it again. It's not worth the risk of being bitten. It's also better to keep the dog under control than it is to have to regain control over a hyped-up animal.

5. Don't make a grab for the animal if it jumps from the table to the floor.

Once on the floor, the dog is on its own, out of control, and able to do whatever it wants. It may well resent your sudden attempt to restrain it. It may interpret your action as aggressive, or as a punishment for jumping.

YOU COULD GET BITTEN!

Instead, immediately command the dog by name—"Pepe, sit!" Be firm, and patient. Don't project excitement in your voice that would excite the dog. Stop him in his tracks with words, before he realizes he's on his own. Follow up the "Sit" command at once with "Stay!" Now assure him that he won't be punished by calling his name and in a gentle tone, praise him for following directions to sit and stay! "Good boy! Good Pepe!"

You may now, cautiously, pick up the dog, return him to the table with a firm command to stay. If the dog rolls over on its back, this is usually interpreted as a sign of submission. Don't believe it! Some animals will fight from this position, using their feet as well as their teeth. The best thing to do is toss a choker leash over him and regain control.

6. Muzzle strong-mouthed, large, or aggressive breeds prior to cutting their nails.

The best of pets will strike the hand that feeds it, if it is suffering pain. At some time or another every groomer will trim the dog's nails a bit too close, draw blood, and inflict unintentional pain. Just as a nurse cannot give an injection without sometimes causing discomfort, so it is with trimming nails, if done properly.

It isn't always good enough to wait to see if you're going to have a problem before muzzling. You may not get the opportunity to put the muzzle on after the animal becomes frightened or aware of the procedure, or your intent. Remember, also, that the purpose of the muzzle is to protect you from injury. It will have done no good to muzzle after you've been bitten.

While some breeds may require some type of restraint for other than the nail clipping procedure, that's usually not the case. However, it's a safe work habit to always muzzle when in doubt. You should never have to work in fear of injury.

When installing a muzzle, you must make sure of two important factors before starting to work the animal. First, be sure it can't slip off easily, giving you a false sense of security. It must be secured in such a way so as to prevent the dog from getting his nails under it and pushing it off. You may also have to restrain the feet to prevent the dog from tearing its own face in the attempt.

Second, you must make sure that the dog is able to breathe freely. An improperly placed tie-around-type muzzle can shut off the air to the pet, constricting the nasal passage if tied too close to the end of the muzzle. Always tie as close to the stop as possible. Don't use a tie muzzle on very short-muzzled dogs such as Shih-tzus and Pekes. For those breeds, a box or cage muzzle should suffice if needed.

The use of a PSDG Clippin' Sling™ provides benefits that overcome much of the problem of having to muzzle short-faced dogs. These breeds usually are short in neck as well as leg. The sling encompasses the neck so well that the use of a restrictive neck collar around it is all that is needed to prevent the dog from striking the hands, when doing the front feet. The dog naturally can't turn in the sling to attack you when working the hind feet either.

Other sensitive areas, such as the tail, anus, face, and ears, may be also worked more safely in the sling due to the absolutely stationary control that can be established. Since the dog can be maintained under control more comfortably, there is less desire for the animals to behave aggressively, allowing you to work all areas safely.

7. Always bend your knees when lifting a heavy dog, or any dog, off the floor.

This piece of good work habit advice has been tried and proved true in all industries for centuries. Lifting properly eliminates strain that would be put on the lower lumbar muscles that could end up in spasm. Having to work a full day with the arms in the air with a backache is something you don't want to experience. A few simple morning calisthenics that include back bends each morning will help eliminate the back pain potential also.

8. Don't wear wooden clogs, open-toed sandals, or high heels in the grooming area.

You'd think this would be an obvious statement. However, many an otherwise intelligent individual has spent their days just asking for trouble by not realizing the potential danger that improper attire can present.

Wooden clogs will slip on any small amount of hair that comes underfoot. Open toes or sandals present a hazard to the instep if an instrument is dropped. High heels may easily catch on the clipper wire and trip the wearer. High heels can also twist the ankle when attempting to lift a larger dog from a low cage on floor.

It is also advisable not to wear large hoop earrings since many dogs will climb on the groomer's shoulder or put their paws there. A paw accidentally slipped into an earring can result in a torn earlobe.

Wear loose-fitting clothing rather than tight restrictive types that make it difficult to bend and breathe. Always dress for the job.

9. Observe good health habits in your work routine.

You can't work a full day and do continuous quality work if you aren't feeling fit. Proper diet, rest and exercise other than that which you get on the job is required. You need good reflexes at times to protect yourself as well as the dog. Keeping late hours without proper rest will dull your senses and judgement. It can cause you to do things in ways you otherwise wouldn't. When you are overtired, you may attempt to take shortcuts that may put you at risk. You lack the proper reflexes that a well-rested mind and body can provide.

Poor eating habits will also rob you of the energy that is required for operating a physically draining business. If you're going to do a full day's worth of groomings, you must have sufficient nourishment to satisfy the demands made of your body. To stay healthy, and not lower your resistance, you must take the time to replenish the muscles with proteins and carbohydrates in sufficient numbers to stave off exhaustion. Don't skip meals on a busy day. It will eventually catch up with you and cost you time, money and discomfort. It may even cost you future good health.

10. Use caution in handling insecticidal shampoos and dips.

Constant exposure even to regular non-insecticidal shampoos and rinses can cause irritation to the hands of some groomers. The oil-cutting action, which causes wetting agents in shampoos to wash clean, can rob the human skin of natural oils that keep it soft.

Repeated exposure without protection to shampoo concentrates and dips can be hazardous. These should be protected against by cautious handling and gloved protection. I've always reduced shampoo concentrates in advance by the gallon for future use for the bathing process. Shampoo concentrate should never be applied directly to the dog and then diluted on the animal, for obvious reasons.

Some shampoos that contain pesticides, and dips designed to kill insects, contain chemicals that can have a cumulative effect on humans. The groomer exposed to some pesticides on a daily basis may react and display symptoms of rash, dizziness, nausea, irritability, poor judgment, and a host of others. Some are carcinogenic. Some reactions may go unnoticed and finally seem to come up suddenly. However, these are due to the cumulative effect some chemicals have. It is up to everyone to determine how he or she wishes to operate. Just as it's almost impossible to make a confirmed smoker stop smoking, some groomers and bathers refuse to wear gloves and protective aprons while working with potentially hazardous materials.

Since some are potentially more hazardous than others, I've always made it a practice to use no pesticide solutions other than those of botanical origin, and predominantly Pyrethrums, extracted from African chrysanthemum flowers.

Always play it safe by not eating or smoking when handling flea- and tick-killing substances. Be sure the area is well ventilated when the vapors from these products are evaporating during the drying process.

After more than 25 years of using Oster Shampoo and Hilo Dip as directed, I am glad to report of never having had a case of animal, instructor or student irritation or medical difficulty, to my knowledge.

11. Don't attempt to eat and groom at the same time.

Besides the stress put on the digestive tract by this practice, it is unsanitary and can be life-threatening.

It is possible to ingest bacteria and a variety of disease organisms due to eating with unclean hands. Let's face it, dogs do have some unclean health habits. They've built a resistance to much of what they're subjected to, but we haven't. Do the wrong thing and you can be infected with salmonella, Lyme disease, or tapeworms, to mention a few. You never know where the dog has been walking just prior to handling his feet, or other areas lacking cleanliness. Keep unwashed hands away from your mouth.

Always wash your hands with a germicidal or antibacterial soap, if possible, before touching your food. Make it a safe working health habit, to stay healthy.

Equipment sanitation and sterilization

One of the easiest ways to maintain a strong client following is by doing all you can to keep the animals healthy. Besides helpful advice that may be given to the client regarding the apparent physical condition, effort should be made to eliminate possibilities of fungus or bacteria buildup and contamination of equipment.

Cages should be routinely washed and disinfected with suitable cleansers to prevent a breeding ground for disease germs.

Tables used in the grooming operation should get the same treatment as cages. Both should be washed with a solution of one tablespoonful of household bleach to a gallon of water to prevent the possible spread of Parvo virus. Parvo is a deadly killer of very young and old canines. Bleach has been found to be the best thing you can use for sanitation and prevention.

Bathing tubs should be sanitized, not just rinsed, at the end of each day. Warm moist areas breed mold, mildew and fungus. Besides the obvious smell produced, there lies a danger of disease germs propagating. Again, a bit of bleach as a final rinse after a thorough scrubbing will eliminate any potential problem.

Hand tools and clipper blades may be sanitized as they are switched from one dog to another with the use of the modern spray sanitizers available.

I have always made it a routine practice to sterilize hand tools by exposing them in a confined cabinet to formaldehyde gas. This is available in tablet form that will allow the gas to form and evaporate in the designated enclosure. This product will give you a method of sterilization that will not rust carbon steel such as scissors and blades are made of. The dry gas permeates all cracks and crevices where spray sanitizers cannot reach.

Caution: Formaldehyde is hazardous. Do not inhale the fumes when placing or retrieving tools.

Shop sanitation

Effective disinfectants and cleaners are imperative to provide a healthy environment for animals and groomers alike. Though the market seems flooded with cleaning solutions, knowing the right one to select for the job required sometimes can be confusing.

Before discussing sanitation needs, a definition of some of the basic terms used will help establish a better understanding of the materials available.

A disinfectant may be termed an antiseptic when it is applied to body tissues. Superficial wounds such as abrasions and minor infections may be treated with antiseptics.

Bacteriostatic means that the organisms are suppressed but may revive and thrive once again.

To disinfect means to eliminate or make free from infection.

A word followed by the suffix "-cidal" means that the material has the ability to kill microorganisms.

Gram negative and gram positive are simply terms used in the lab to distinguish a group of bacteria from each other. Positive retains the dye used on the slide, negative does not.

There are many good cleaning agents and disinfectants available on the market that have the best properties of both contained in one solution. These are laboratory combinations, constructed to be compatible with each other. It is wise not to try to formulate your own mixture of disinfectant and cleaning agent. You could create a combination that renders each component ineffective, regardless how much you may use.

One of the disinfectants readily available is alcohol. It has the special benefit of being able to dehydrate, evaporates quickly, and is bactericidal against many gram negative-type bacteria. Both ethyl and isopropyl-type alcohol are beneficial. Ethyl at 70% solution is most desirable, but isopropyl, rubbing alcohol, at 85% solution is about as effective. Both are particularly effective in moist conditions where some water is present.

For organisms that are common and non-spore-producing, 40% ethyl will be effective in most conditions. Both alcohols have little action against bacterial or fungal spores. Some spores of fungal origin will succumb after several minutes' exposure. It is for this reason we don't want to intentionally dry the feet after alcohol swabbing.

Blades or other hand tools that are to be sterilized with alcohol solutions or sprays must be cleaned of all foreign matter to be effective. Ethyl alcohol at 70% strength can be a better sterilizer than heat on cutting instruments, provided they are materially clean.

One of the most commonly used disinfectants in use in the industry is chlorhexidine. It is highly virucidal and more effective than most other common germicides in the presence of foreign matter, blood, etc. It is bactericidal against gram negative bacteria but just falls short of laboratory requirements that require it to be 100% absolute to be rated bactericidal against gram positive bacteria. At the usual concentration of gram positive normally found in the field, chlorhexidine is more effective then most other bactericides used in the presence of foreign organic matter.

Chlorhexidine has been found to be fungicidal in specific controlled laboratory tests. Worth noting is that, properly used, it has the least potential of being poisonous of all disinfectants and is noncorrosive to metals or plastics, is effective in hard water and with soaps, and has fairly good residual effectiveness. It is a fine product to use for general table maintenance. Used in a spray bottle, it becomes a handy way to disinfect tub, cage and table surfaces.

When followed with a solution of common household chlorine bleach, which is highly fungicidal as well as virucidal, you have a deadly bactericidal duo that combats Parvo virus as well as other organisms. Enzyme surface sprays are designed to be used after cleaning, and continue to attack organic odor-causing absorbed material until neutralized.

Properly used on a regular basis, these products can keep your shops work surfaces clean-smelling and free from disease-causing germs.

How to practice your new skills

The best tool is of value only when it is being used. Left too long without use, it will become so rusty that it will take considerable work to put it in the same condition as when it was fresh and new.

You will never lose an acquired skill. It is part of what happens when you go through the learning process. Your mind becomes programmed like a computer. It waits for you to touch the right thought button and then it springs back into action. It doesn't matter if it has been months or years.

Roller skating, bike riding, dog grooming — these are all acquired skills. No one is born with them. You never lose them once learned.

However, that skill might need a bit of oiling if it has been allowed to rust for some time. It can stay sharply honed only through continued use or "practice."

Many new groomers start on their own dogs, if they have them. When their skills become known, it seems that the family members come out of the woodwork, offering their animals for a chance to save a grooming fee. Before long neighbors get into the act and a regular grooming schedule is established. That is one way to practice your grooming, and some have done it successfully; a slow but sure method. After a bit, if the clients are satisfied with the grooming, a small business comes into being due to the word-of-mouth advertising received, courtesy of those satisfied clients. More about advertising later.

Another way you may practice your new skills is to offer them to facilities who could use them. Pet shops who offer grooming, boarding and grooming kennels, grooming salons, and veterinarians are in need of assistance at various times of the year. Either on a part-time or full-time basis, many school graduates make their start this way.

Still another way to practice your skills is to work at being a home groomer. Naturally, all laws pertaining to business operation should be adhered to. A home groomer is one who grooms in the client's own home. Business is done on location, without the use of your own shop. Certain benefits and of course drawbacks are obtained and encountered.

There will be no rent, electricity, heat, or water to pay for. No sanitation, or maintenance costs or repairs to make, either. There will be transportation costs, auto expenses such as the automobile itself, insurance, gas, oil, and wear and tear maintenance for tires, brakes, and state inspections.

The grooming equipment, including a portable folding table and hand dryer, is transported from one home location to another, on a regular grooming schedule. Some groomers successfully operate by having the client prebathe the animal so that the groomer's time is conserved. A discount is usually allowed that is well worth giving for a busy schedule.

Some of the negative aspects of this method of doing business are as follows:

- Clients sometimes forget their appointments. You may make the trip to their home for nothing. Eliminate this possibility by telephoning ahead just prior to making the trip. Even so, they might be walking the dog or shopping just prior to your call or arrival. It is a constant education problem.

- The groomer may arrive only to find that the dog is outside, and won't come in, or runs upstairs and under the bed and can't be coaxed out — a real waste of the groomer's time. This may be counteracted by a service charge of half the grooming price being assessed in the event the client cannot produce the dog for grooming in a reasonable amount of time. This naturally must be preestablished.

- The groomer may arrive at a new client's home only to encounter a snarling, snapping, 85-pound vicious animal that the client said was a 25-pound angel. Whether intentionally or by miscalculation, the time is lost, and so is the fee. Better to bow out gracefully than to risk severe injury on the animal's home turf. You will receive no reward for bravery in the doctor's office.

- Another scenario is when an animal reacts O.K. but the client insists on "watching so the dog will behave." Naturally, the effect is just the opposite. The client's distracting presence may make an easy job difficult. The client may refuse to allow you to muzzle when you know you should for safety. Their constant conversation itself can break your concentration, causing accident and injury.

Of course, there is no perfect approach to any business; they all have good and bad aspects. It is up to each individual to appraise the possibilities and choose what is best suited for them. Whatever the choice, it will be superior to doing nothing for fear of trying. Your skill can only improve and serve you when put into practice.

Opening a grooming salon

To many, opening a grooming salon of their own is the culmination of their grooming education: a place to practice their skills that may become known to the public as a good place to obtain grooming service is far from a far-fetched dream. It is within the grasp of anyone who can groom well and has a feel for business operation as well. A double-edged sword that can be rewarding and demanding, running a business of your own accounts for more than the lion's share of the grooming fee. It also is a definite responsibility that will increase as the business does. But for those who try and succeed, there are few if any regrets.

Obtain a property

The first order of business is to obtain a property from which to operate. The three main things that affect the rental or sale price of a commercial property, it has been said, are location, location and location.

Your first place of business need not be so large or so well located that simply paying the rent becomes the chief reason for you to do business. Remember, it is your skill and the way you handle your clients that matters. Properly done, your clients will patronize you in a modest clean shop. Poorly done, the largest shopping mall wouldn't be good enough. Clients travel many miles, passing other shops to get to the one that offers quality work on a professional basis, regardless of the shop's size.

A grooming shop need not be located in a shopping mall or center to do a good steady business. Many a successful business has been started in a small neighborhood store.

Speak to a real estate agent and keep on the lookout for a SMALL place. My first location was an enclosed 8′ × 12′ greenhouse on the side of a building, and I was doing 10 dogs a day there. There was not even a bathroom; I had to use the gas station across the street. The shoe repair shop next door allowed me to tap their water line and hook up a Sears plastic stationary tub for bathing in my "shop." I didn't even have a sign outside; word of mouth directed clients to me. It was a mixed zone neighborhood, semi-residential. But it *was* a start!

Remember that *your* ideal shop and location may be what every other business *doesn't* want. It can be off the beaten path, even behind a store or a shared portion of a pet shop. As a skilled grooming technician, *you'll draw clients to it!* And you can rent—you don't have to buy the property. It can be very small. My second shop was less than 300 square feet, and I groomed 15 dogs a day there. In a pet shop, don't offer to share more than 20% of the grooming bill as payment for rent, electricity, heat, etc., because you'll draw business in for the shop for pet supplies that it wouldn't otherwise get.

Naturally, these points are always negotiable, based perhaps on the store's agreeing to a sales commission on any supplies that are purchased as a result of your suggestion and efforts.

You run the grooming concession, so KEEP ALL THE CLIENT RECORDS UNDER LOCK AND KEY OR TAKE THE FILE HOME WITH YOU EACH NIGHT. Advertise for and *make your own appointments* for all clients. Have a written agreement that you are an independent agent and that ALL GROOMING RECORDS REMAIN YOUR EXCLUSIVE PROPERTY.

Remember the number of dogs that must be groomed each month to pay the property rent or lease. You will be less likely to overextend yourself in selection of your first location.

Regardless of where you locate, always obtain a minimal lease with an option, if possible. This will allow you to stay at the location after expiration of the lease period (usually one year) if you want to. You may also move to a new location without penalty. This option will allow you to continue to rent for the number of years previously established, and if you restate what the rent for the additional years is to be, there won't be any surprises either. Your rent can't be increased any more than the amount originally bargained for.

With an option, you need not worry if you will be allowed to rent for additional years, and for how much. The lease option so designed might appear as follows: "It is agreed that the first years rent shall be x dollars per month with an option to continue for x additional years at x dollars per month for the first renewal year and then x dollars per month for the second year, third year, etc."

Another method of predetermining the inevitable rent increase is to state in the lease a percentage to be applied each year of the exercised option; e.g., "and a 6% increase monthly added each year of the renewed lease till expiration." Or you might state that the increase will be equal to the national cost of living increase. Don't expect a decrease, but don't be ashamed to ask for one at the end of the first year if the location doesn't meet your expectations.

You can suggest a lowered rental as an incentive to exercising your option for an extended lease period. Many times if you negotiate you can come out a winner. You'll never know if you don't try!

Before signing the initial lease, if it is agreeable, have someone familiar with property rental look it over for you. If you feel capable due to previous experience you can skip this step. However, an experienced person can determine if the lease could be drawn to better your interests.

Standard leases are constructed for the renter's benefit. Much can be omitted and amended prior to signing that will make the lease easier to live with. An experienced person or an attorney can point these things out to you. Naturally your rental agent must agree, but that is what negotiation is all about.

Obtain insurance

If renting from the property owner, ask if there is a paid-up policy on the plate glass, when does it expire, and the name of the company. Plate glass is expensive, and you will need insurance coverage. An existing policy can save you time and trouble obtaining one. Ask the company if it can be combined with a business package liability policy. You may get a better rate that way, and you will need liability coverage anyway.

Your liability policy will protect you from lawsuits in the event a client slips on your sidewalk or floor, or trips over her own or another's leash in your shop. A care, custody, and control rider will protect you if the dog escapes from your shop, or is accidentally injured. You need this type of insurance to allow you to sleep peacefully at night. A lawsuit against you could mount into the thousands of dollars. The time, cost, and trouble it could create are enough to put you out of business, or make you wish you weren't in it. Don't take the chance. Get all the insurance coverages you need and relax and enjoy yourself.

Register your business name

After settling the insurance questions, register with the county and state if required to establish the business operating name by which you will be known. It must be recorded and advertised in a legal newspaper in order to obtain a business license in most states. Your city hall's prothonotary office or your accountant can advise you further regarding the local laws in your area.

Open a business bank account

Once you have an official business name, open a bank account in that name and from that point on, use your business checks to make payment for all that pertains to the business. All deposits for utilities, rents, supplies, materials, and contractors should be recorded in your checkbook. This will be the basis of the exemptions you will be entitled to at tax time.

Either you or your accountant will refer to your check record for profit and loss determination as well. If you want the exemption benefit of being in business, you must be able to prove the expense by having a record.

If you will be using a delivery vehicle, be sure to make associated payments for gas, oil, repairs, and insurance with your business check to claim a valid deduction. Naturally, you must also keep a record of miles driven in a daily diary.

Contact utility companies

Establish an account with utility companies. You will need electricity to set up your shop right from the start. You or your hired contractors will need light to paint by and power to operate tools for construction. You will need an air conditioner to keep the heat and humidity at a comfortable level. Drying dogs will produce moisture that must be removed to prevent mildew and odor in your shop. If practical, purchase an air conditioner larger in size than needed to accommodate the constant load that will be put on it by both dogs and dryers.

Install an exhaust fan in the rear of your shop. Excess moisture accumulates from wet bath surfaces and wet towels that may be allowed to evaporate dry in the shop overnight. An exhaust fan will take the strain off the air conditioner. It will air out your shop first thing in the morning so it smells clean and fresh for your morning clients. It will also be valuable for those times when Fifi has an unscheduled nature call.

Arrange for a business phone

Obtain a business phone and have a paper preopening sign lettered with the phone number on it. Install it in your shop window. Advise on the sign the approximate opening date and that "appointments are now being accepted." In that way you will have business coming in the very day you plan to open. What could look better for a new business?

An answering service or machine to take the calls when you are busy grooming will preserve your business, and keep you from losing any.

Keep your machine, if you use one, on monitor within hearing distance from where your grooming station is. In that way, if a call comes in desiring grooming that day, and you have an opening, you may reply at once and secure the job. Other calls may be returned when you are not busy grooming. Be sure to return calls at your first opportunity or you may lose new clients anxious to have their new puppy groomed.

When, where and how to advertise

Advertising doesn't cost, it pays, or so they say. In my experience, good, well-designed ads in the proper media, placed at the proper time, for the proper price, can, in fact, "pay."

Advertising comes in many forms, some of which are too seldom considered and therefore overlooked. These can be your best forms of letting the public know who you are and what you can do for them. That, after all, is the purpose of advertising. Poor advertising can be worse than none at all, so thought should be given before broadcasting your message to the public.

A badly worded ad placed in the right media can be misleading, can misinform and cause potential clients to turn off. A well-constructed ad placed in the wrong place can cost a bundle but produce little in return. A well-placed ad, well constructed, but too expensive, can cause you to work just to pay off the ad, with no profit forthcoming in the near future.

The best form of advertising need cost you nothing! It comes from your satisfied clients. A testimonial is more believable coming from a current client than all the wordage that may be used in a newspaper ad. And talk about cost-effective — what could be better than free? Here's why:

One client who is proud of her pooch's well-groomed looks may tell two other dog owners, who give you a try. Satisfy them and each one may tell two, and so on. Automatically your business starts to increase, without added cost. Of course, it's a good idea to ask your new clients who might have referred them to you. You can then show your appreciation by sending a thank-you card, or present a small gift at time of the next grooming. This small amount of effort can induce the client to continue efforts on your behalf.

The next least expensive form of advertising comes from the proper use of business cards. Usually, one presents a card when one is requested, or when introducing oneself for the first time to a prospect.

When I first went into the grooming business as a small shop operator, I employed a method of business-building advertising using business cards in a novel way. The method is just as applicable today as it was over 25 years ago. Although this method may not be to every groomer's taste, I recommend it strongly, for those with limited capital, who wish to get a jump start for a new business. Here's what to do:

Have your printer produce a quantity (usually 1,000 is the minimum) of good-quality business cards printed professionally in two colors. Be sure to have an attractive picture of at least one dog on the card. This may be a photo or illustration; either is fine. Besides your business name, address (if desired) and phone number (mandatory), also list the services you provide. This might include clipping, bathing, dipping, nail cutting, custom styles, polish and bows.

While your cards are being printed, make note of all the places in your area that have long grassy strips running alongside the walkways. These may be parks, churches, schools, driveways — wherever a dog owner might be in the habit, good or bad as it may be, of walking the dog. Then try this!

When your cards are received, get up early one morning and take a ride or walk around those prenoted areas. About 7am is the right time to be there. Now, when an owner is walking his pet pooch, approach him with hand outstretched, card in hand, and simply say, "I have something for your doggie here!" Just hand over the card and be on your way. Don't stop to talk or you will defeat the purpose. You want to spend time distributing cards, not talking. Here's what eventually happens.

You've had the chance to see the type, size, and service needs of the dog being walked. You can decide if that is the type you wish to work on. You get the owner thinking about grooming, and place your ad in his hand, and he usually pockets it for future use. One day, the prospective client's own groomer may be booked or sick, go out of business, relocate to a less convenient area, or even die. The client may be dissatisfied with his present groomer's last job, or just be fickle and want to try someone else.

At this point, he remembers the card pocketed and phones you! "I was walking my dog and someone gave me your business card," is the usual opening statement made. You have been able to secure a new client at a cost of about two cents for the card. One new client's service pays for the total lot of cards, and then some.

You will be amazed at how, by just extending your hand, dog owners are willing to accept your card when you say it is for their dog. It's good business builder, and you know for sure that those you want to see your ad are going to.

The most constant form of advertising

Although the initial cost monthly is far from inexpensive, for constancy you cannot beat the Yellow Pages phone directory. The reason is simple. Your ad is always there for those who are seeking a groomer and don't have any other source of information. No matter when they look, it is there. When they just acquire that new puppy from the shelter or pet shop and want it cleaned up prior to taking it home, your ad is there.

When they become dissatisfied with their present groomer or cannot get the appointed date they are after, your ad is there to direct them to you. Unlike any other form of advertising, including radio, TV, and newspapers, the Yellow Pages directory doesn't require timely attention in order to be a reference.

Another reason is that it is indexed. Where in the newspaper can you get direction as to where a display ad you have placed is located? It has to be stumbled upon to be noticed! On the other hand, the Yellow Pages has a specific Pet Washing and Grooming section that is easy to find, and is always available to the inquiring client, new or old.

There are certain requirements the company insists on before running a Yellow Pages ad. You must be a company that has its name registered with the county, state, or both. You must have an assigned business telephone number. Specific size ads are required in order to accept some desired ad material, borders, logos, etc. And, of course, you must keep your credit good or risk loss of your business telephone service, if you have purchased the phone company's own Yellow Pages service.

The cost of this form of advertising can be expensive if you are not doing sufficient business to cover it. It would be very foolhardy for a new grooming venture to commit to a large ad that must be paid for 12 months prior to proving the business could support it.

The key to doing this type of advertising is for a small new operation to move slowly and prove the ability as well as the requirement for running an ad that might otherwise prove a burden. Properly done, your ad will be a constant silent productive salesman.

Changeable type advertising

Whereas business cards and phone book ads are static during the life of the printing of the card lot, or book contract, timely information such as specials cannot be made known to the public in this way. These, therefore, must be allocated to fast-changing media. Newspapers, local shopper guides, circulars, ad bulletins, cooperative ad circulars, and coupon ad envelope packets are all in this category.

Newspapers can be far-reaching, and, depending on the size of the paper, may extend out of the business area you are hoping to penetrate. Look for area editions to place your ad in, within a 30-to-40-mile radius. Look for most of your business to come from there. Your ad may look good in an edition that sells 100 miles from your shop, but will draw little business from there, and you are paying for the privilege of advertising there. Most large city newspapers have various in-city sections as well. It then is possible to pinpoint the area you want exposure in by citing your desire to the sales representative.

Smaller local newspapers have a twofold benefit. They cost less to advertise in due to a more limited circulation, and because of their smaller number of pages, your display ad is more likely to be seen by the reader. If it's local clientele you are looking to influence, these papers usually carry many neighborhood news articles that attract them to the pages.

Don't overlook the classified section as a good place for your current message. Many people scan this section quickly who don't read other portions of the paper. It is less expensive than run of the paper display ads, and gets the same amount of circulation benefit. In some papers, the classified section runs in all editions, giving you wider coverage at the same price.

Newspaper ads may be run on an individual basis, or on contract for a certain number of lines per year. Contracts give you a better price. You naturally are obligated to the contract as you would be with a phone directory, but you can change your ad each week if you see fit to.

Newspapers inform people where you are, even if they don't go looking for you, as in a phone book. Of course, when they see your ad they may not be ready for your service. The way to make your ad "live" past its issue date is to make it valuable in some way. Here is one way to do it.

Design a broken line border around the ad to give it a coupon appearance. In the body of the ad, advise that a "free gift for new clients will be given when this ad is presented at time of grooming." This could be a small toy or rawhide bone giveaway. Your offer will cause those who may want to bring their dog in at a later date to clip the coupon and thereby retain your shop's name and phone number. Otherwise, it may be forgotten and not recalled when service is desired by a new prospect. An expiration date encourages action, and can induce business during a designated time period.

Miscellaneous forms of ad placement

The same principles may be applied to area shopper booklets and coupon packs. The outcome of this medium of advertising unfortunately depends on how it circulates. Usually shoppers are distributed to large chain stores with the hope that the customers will pick them up. Many are just dumped in the trash by irresponsible delivery persons, especially those being delivered in some areas to homes that never reach them.

Coupon packs are normally contracted for in advance and are not as easy to make timely. However, they are usually sent through the mail. You know that they are getting into the homes. Coupon packs are also known as piggy back advertising. Your ad coupon will be mailed with other types of coupons in the one unit envelope.

Tips for speed, safety, and professionalism

According to Webster, a profession is "a calling requiring specialized knowledge, usually participated in for financial gain." The word professional has been used in connection with other activities such as sports, to divide those who are so-called amateurs because they receive no compensation for their activities and in most cases haven't perfected their talents. Most often a vision of a doctor or lawyer is conjured up when one mentions a "professional." Certainly they have obtained specialized knowledge, and most do have a calling for their life's work, but so do many others in other fields. Doctors and lawyers have, however, elevated their "profession" to a point where they command the respect of their clients as a result of demonstrated abilities, but even more due to their ability to quickly analyze and diagnose a situation prior to the application of their physical and mental talents. Once analyzed, they take over the situation and remain in command until its conclusion. So it must be in our profession in order to be respected and successful.

The following proven ideas will help you to gain that degree of speed, while retaining safe control that keeps you in command of the situation, as a true professional.

Client reception

The reception or taking in of the pet for grooming can be a most critical phase of the grooming process. If done correctly it can be a step toward establishing your professionalism, and the cement that can bind the client to the groomer for the life of the pet.

It is important to review your records of each expected client prior to their arrival with their pet. In this way you may recognize the clients by the breed, color, size, sex, etc., of their pet and be prepared to discuss the days service with them. Any critical information should be noted on the client's records in red. That way you'll spot it immediately and avoid appearing uninformed of a condition previously discussed. This will also save time and keep you in command of the situation.

It isn't enough to have records; you must also examine the client's pet each time it is presented for grooming.

If your clients know you're concerned about the dog's health and the condition of its coat, then they will attach more importance to it also. The amount of time lapsed since the previous grooming, the amount of care and attention to brushing and combing, and flea control will vary from client to client. It will also vary with the same client from one time to another. An accurate record can give you a hint of what to expect, but only by complete examination will you know what the true conditions are. Then you can analyze, diagnose and prescribe a proper solution for a client's request.

For example, a matted coat, one that cannot be combed out, will require the complete removal of the coat close to the skin line. Regardless what the client may want in the way of styling, that is what must be done. The groomer must be quick to reach this conclusion and advise the client of same. By demonstrating the severity of the matting with a comb, it will be easier to get the client's agreement as to the condition. With this agreement will also come the approval to get on with the job that must be done. Again, you will have retained command of the situation by your professional approach.

Delivery of the groomed pet

Being able to deliver or have ready a client's pet when promised will have a great effect on a groomer's business. We have all experienced the disappointment of being on time for an appointment, or for a pickup of a repaired item, only to find that we had to wait, or worse yet, come back later. It is hard to maintain confidence in someone whom you cannot count on. When a pet isn't ready on time as promised, a client may also worry that something has happened to the animal. Even if everything is O.K., the client won't be until the dog is presented healthy and happy. That period of anxiety doesn't help build accounts.

At times the client may come in for pickup early. It helps to have the pet ready and waiting a bit earlier than promised so it can go home immediately. Once the owner's scent is detected by the dog, it becomes harder to control it for finishing. The heating or air conditioning system will carry the owner's unique scent through the ductwork and back to wherever the dog is being worked on, sometimes putting them in a frenzy, making it hard to control and finish.

Although not all professionals are on time, the better thought-of ones are.

Appointments

The way you schedule an appointment depends upon whom you are working with. An obviously ill-cared-for pet, extremely matted, whom the client seems to have little regard for, more likely than not will not return in six weeks for a grooming if the coat had to be clipped off close.

To give an appointment to such a client would eliminate the possibility of another client's being scheduled for that slot, and would be a waste of potential income. If, however, your appointment book has not reached working capacity, go ahead and book anyone that has even the slightest potential of showing up. You have nothing to lose, and may gain.

Booking too far ahead can also mislead you as to what you can count on for the day. Nothing is as annoying as having turned down a client for grooming on a day that appears to be at capacity, only to find that the client who was "booked" six months ago has forgotten her appointment. The answer to the problem is simply don't book at long range unless you take the time to remind the client the week of the appointment. A postcard, or a phone call early in the day, will greatly decrease the number of no-shows in your business. Of course, there are exceptions to all situations, but in most cases it is best to have long-distance appointments be confirmed by the client, the week the appointment is due. They do forget.

When selling appointments by telephone for dogs not yet groomed, always attempt to fill the fore part of the week first, giving yourself more time to fill the latter days of the week. Usually, Saturday will take care of itself.

If you do not intend to operate your grooming business in the evening, you will need Saturdays for those working clients who won't be able to appoint any other day. The secret of successful booking is simply not to allow the client to dictate the day of appointment to you. Instead, you must suggest the day you desire to groom the client's dog based upon your work load. You will usually have no problem if you suggest that your next opening is on Thursday, for instance. If not satisfactory, your client will tell you and then you are free to suggest another date.

Key points to remember during the grooming process

Grooming control is the main factor that allows the professional to accomplish each procedure in a safe speedy way. When control becomes habit, confidence as well as speed is the premium result. The following is a list of check points to remember to avoid control difficulties and accidents.

a. Always keep the dog seated, unless it is necessary to have it standing for a particular procedure.

b. Keep the skin tight when brushing, combing, or clipping to avoid injury to wrinkled skin.

c. Keep the web areas tucked in with the control hand fingers when working near these areas.

d. When working around the anal area, hold the tail in a full hand grasp, little finger next to spine, with the thumb being uppermost. Keep your elbow down for greater strength to support a dog that attempts to sit while working this area.

e. Protect dewclaw toes from being torn when combing or clipping by holding them in your grasp while working this area.

f. Occasionally check blade temperature and use spray coolant as needed.

g. Underbelly work should be done with a cool blade using light flicking touches with full edge contact. Do not use blade corners in deep pocket areas.

h. Before doing any kind of work in or on delicate or critical areas, give a strong "Stay" command in a firm tone, obtain control, and keep the dog reminded through repetition.

i. If the dog lies down and is required to stand, first bring it to a seated position by placing one hand under the lower jaw in a muzzle grip while the other hand remains on the rump. Lift the dog up with the jaw hand until its front legs are straight and its feet touch the table. Next, grasp one hind leg and lift the dog's rear up until the leg not being held straightens and the foot touches the table. Use your free hand to steady the dog and then lower the held leg to the table to stand on all fours. The total process is accomplished while standing behind the dog. Never attempt to bring the dog to a standing position by grabbing with two hands under the belly and lifting to all four feet at once.

j. With the dog seated, never crank the head back to a 90-degree angle or more. Try to maintain between 45 and 70 degrees so the dog may breathe easily.

k. Lower the dog's head occasionally when working with the head lifted back to allow the dog to swallow, but do not release the muzzle grip until the procedure is completed.

l. When clipping or shaving over face, be sure the blade spans the lips so that the blade hasn't a chance of sliding into and catching the corner of the mouth.

m. Before shaving lower eyelids, be sure no long eyelashes are protruding that will be picked up by the blade drawing the lid into it. If required, trim lashes with scissors first, then shave lower lids with a cool blade.

n. Trim long heavy whiskers with scissors prior to clipping or shaving in order to avoid pulling, which will cause the dog not to hold in control, and it may refuse to allow a second attempt at the procedure.

o. Never shave ears with the blade overlapping the edge running parallel to the edge. Always shave perpendicular to the edge, off the edge.

p. Use great care when shaving the head at the ear base to avoid cutting the incline of the ear.

q. When shaving inside ears, employ positive control and use extreme care at cartilage area at ear opening. Do not shave against and behind it.

r. Always hold cartilage with the thumb and middle finger to dilate the ear when working inside with forceps.

s. When applying Klip-Klot®, always pack into the nail quick by *twisting with your thumb and applying pressure* to the seal below the surface, after application.

t. Always muzzle or restrain the head on Terriers or aggressive breeds before cutting nails.

u. Hold the mouth shut when shaving or clipping the face to keep the tongue inside to avoid injury.

v. Determine if the tail bone ends in a hook before brushing, combing, or clipping that area.

w. Keep an alcohol-soaked swab handy when working on dogs suspected of fleas to suppress same.

x. Watch the clock to maintain the proper pace and relieve the stress that comes with a last-minute rush to finish.

y. Resist the temptation to make desperation scissor cuts when the dog is not in control.

z. Never scissor-trim hair behind fingers that are holding in a pinch grip. Always trim forward of the gripping fingers.

Always check the blade number or type when picking up a clipper with blade installed before using it on your dog. Never assume that it is the right one.

Equipment requirements

Experienced groomers realize that the world's best equipment, in unskilled hands, will still produce less than a quality job. It is also true that few of us can afford the world's best of everything, nor is it required to do a good job.

Good quality equipment in the hands of a skilled groomer can produce excellent results. You can compromise on price, but not on quality.

Clippers

These are the heart of your equipment requirement and were previously discussed in the clipping instructions. The best have a detachable blade and a variety of blades to select from.

They should be comfortable in the hand and shaped so that they are easily manipulated with one hand as the other controls the dog. The inner parts should be easily accessed so that they may be maintained with minimum effort and cost.

No professional grooming operator should be established without a minimum of two clippers on hand. In the event of malfunction or accidental damage, you must have another to complete your day's work.

Both revenue and reputation are at stake when animals must be sent home un-groomed. I have always made it a rule not to accept any animal I thought I might not be able to finish, and to finish, no matter what, every animal I had accepted.

A sufficient amount of spare equipment is in itself an insurance that you cannot well afford to be without. For that reason, you should maintain a working stock of at least three of each clipper blade you will be using in business. One blade will be the one that you will work with. The second blade of the same type will be reserved to use when your first blade goes dull and needs sharpening. The third blade, of the same type, will be reserved in the event that your second blade is dropped and breaks or goes dull while the first is being sharpened. In this way you will never be without the equipment you require.

Scissors

There are almost as many varieties of scissors, also called shears, as there are dogs. Many will choose a particular type depending upon the breed they wish to groom and the results they are trying to attain. If small to medium-sized dogs are to be groomed, a 7″ to 8″ scissor length will be sufficient. Of course, these may also be used for the larger long-coated breeds, but you will sacrifice speed and efficiency. It becomes a matter of personal preference. I have always preferred the 7″ length to the other sizes. The larger ones seemed unwieldy and the smaller styling scissor unsuitable for my method of trimming.

Straight pointed scissors

These are the type most human barbers use. They are useful to trim pattern lines and areas where shave lines are desired to show sharp delineation from the body coat. They are great for trim lines around shaven Poodle-style feet. The sharp points allow for close skin contact and clean-looking lines.

I always restricted the use of this type of scissors for the above stated work on most breeds due to my concern for the safety aspect of grooming. Sharp points can easily injure puppies and nervous pets even if the groomer is conscientious. The slightest eye contact with such scissors will easily injure the cornea, at the very least. A sudden lunge can cause penetration of the abdomen or injury to the genital areas. I always preferred to play it safe by using a safer variety for general trim work.

Blunt tip curved scissors

These are available in both stainless steel and carbon steel, with permanent or replaceable blades, as are pointed scissors. Replaceable blades are at time of this writing available only in stainless for the 7″ scissors.

The blunt tip is ball-shaped and protects delicate areas from accidental penetration. The curve forged into the blades provides a slight automatic contour when trimming areas requiring it. This makes it the ideal scissor for trimming head and leg pompoms. Once gotten used to, it is hard to conceive of using a straight scissor for these areas, or why one would want to.

This shear is used with the tip pointing toward the animal when establishing a rounded contour, and away from the body when a straight line is desired, by using the first half of the scissor. When curved lines and bevels are desired, the blades are simply held in position to match the contour, such as the bottom of the tassel of the ear.

Good scissoring speed can be made using this type of scissor, with less concern for stab-type injuries, due to the blunt ball-shaped tips.

Both carbon and stainless steel scissors require periodic sharpening. While replaceable blades are available for stainless scissors built to take them, there aren't any made for carbon steel types. Replaceable blades can also be sharpened, so spare sets can be kept on hand and switched when the ones in use become dull. In either case, the blade edges will grasp and hold the hair more efficiently for cutting if the edges are serrated. This procedure is done after the sharpening process. It simply consists of drawing a mill file over the edge at the same angle sharpened to cut fine grooves in it. With practice, on an old pair of shears, the average handy groomer can learn to keep the edge dressed and avoid much of the resharpening expense and inconvenience associated with the equipment.

Care should be exercised not to drop the finely adjusted scissors lest you knock the set or "bow" from its position of blade-to-blade contact. If this is done, even the sharpest possible scissors will not cut due to the blades not mating. For this reason, never use your good scissors for letter opening or flea collar cutting, if you wish to preserve their good cutting ability. If a moisture-laden dog must be trimmed, be sure to wipe off and oil lightly the blade areas so they don't rust, corrode, or stain due to the wet deposit.

I do not advocate a large variety of scissors, but spares are a must for the same reasons as previously stated concerning clipper blades.

Scissor tension is best adjusted with a scissor press or plier. This tool, easily obtained and operated, allows pressure to be applied while the tightening screw is adjusted. The scissor should just about close all the way when one blade is allowed to drop against the other. This is then evidence that the blade bow is making contact all the way down the blade length. Both straight and curved scissors have a set bow for efficient cutting.

In no case will the scissor determine the finished look of the dog, but it will be an asset to your own skill if handled and cared for properly.

Other coat styling equipment

Thinners, strippers, and shedding blades are all used to achieve a particular coat appearance without the use of electric clippers. Coat condition is the prime consideration when deciding to use these tools. A certain knack must be developed to use them properly and at the right time of the shedding cycle in the case of stripping combs.

For the most part, these tools are reserved for the Terrier breeds, although thinners may be used as required on any long-coated breed.

Stripping, also called plucking in some circles, refers to extracting the dead hair coat from the body. The proper time to do this is when the coat has started to shed. It will appear to explode away from the body as it sheds, hence the term which is often used, "blowncoat."

To provide a better grip on the hair, a magnesium carbonate block or French chalk is first applied to the coat. Small amounts of hair are grasped between the thumb and stripping comb, the same way one would cut a slice of apple with a knife while holding it in the opposite hand. The hair is steadily pulled out in the direction it grows, *with the grain,* working a small area at a time, with patience. If the coat is in the right shedding stage, stripping will be easily accomplished.

After the first stripping, a regular schedule should be maintained, as should be with any type of grooming. By adhering to schedule, stripping should not be a painful process. Once properly done, you can determine the number of weeks till the next stripping by the hair growth, and the regular schedule will be established. Usual brushing and combing should still be given between stripping sessions.

It should be noted that most owners of pet quality breeds opt to have their dogs clipped, to save the added cost of hand stripping.

A shedding blade resembles a bent hacksaw blade, with a leather handle holding it in a bent loop position. It is used to clean out shorter coats that are in the shedding stage. The teeth of the blade are drawn over the coat *with the grain,* and the dead hair extracted as the teeth engage it.

Thinning shears are either single- or double-sided. They are made with a skip slot down the full length of one or both sides of the shear. The purpose is to be able to cut alternating sections of hair to reduce the density and bulk.

Thinning shears are available from coarse to fine finish as determined by the number of teeth contained in the tool. The more teeth, the finer the finish. The tip end of each tooth is notched to hold the hair on the end of it so that it may be cut. The hair that falls between the teeth remains long. This tool is best used close to the skin to produce a more natural look to the area being reduced.

By using thinners at the end of the hair, a less tailored look can be effected to those dogs that you wish to have a "cobby look." Skirt lines and feather ends appear more natural than when trimmed with conventional scissors.

Brushes

While not quite as varied as scissors, there is a large selection of both type and size. Size allows you to get the job done quicker on large breeds and more delicately on smaller ones. Some are handled, and some made to put your hand in.

Of greatest importance to the groomer is the slicker. These rubber-padded brushes have scores of closely spaced, short bent wire pins embedded in them. Their construction makes them unequalled for brushing out knotted and matted coats.

By brushing *against the grain* of the coat, the bristles (wires) penetrate down next to the skin where the dead and dying hair accumulates to form a heavy mat if allowed to. The short stiff curved wires lift up and out, bringing the dead undercoat with them.

This brush is also invaluable when clipping the coat. Reverse brushing causes the coat to stand up so that efficient, even clipping is possible.

When trimming, the slicker's close dense pin construction allows the groomer to draw out and position the hair for accurate scissoring.

Brushes of wood or plastic handle construction, with metal rods about one inch in length in a rubber pad, are called pin brushes. These are fine to use on long-haired dogs in good coat condition. The "pins" have less tendency to damage the ends of the hair than slickers. They are ideal for positioning an already well-brushed coat, but they will not remove mats and tangles as well as a slicker.

Some pin brushes are made double-sided. One side contains pins and the other hair bristles. Some brushes are oval in shape with a leather strap designed for hand insertion. These bristle brushes are ideal for short-haired dogs, and the brushing provides good coat stimulation and helps spread natural oils, producing a glossy coat.

Most other brushes are varieties of the above, either in size, construction, shape, or in combinations.

Dryers for hand, table, and floor use

These units specifically designed for grooming are available in two major type groups. The most used type is designed to blow forced hot air to dry and style the coat. These units may be simple handheld dryers similar to human styling tools. Other types are designed to be attached to cages or kennels to dry the freshly bathed dog contained therein.

Floor model dryers, which are larger, more powerful units, are also made with tube extensions so that they may be connected to drying cages. Some have multiple outlets.

These are mounted on casters so they may be rolled from place to place as they are needed. They have an adjustable height stand and a swivel nozzle. Most have a temperature control to adjust the range of heat required. This type is usually used for styling large dogs standing on tables. The method known as fluff drying, brushing as the hot air is directed into the coat at the area being brushed, is easily accomplished with this type of dryer.

The second group of drying tools are forced air units, which rely on high-velocity evaporation to dry the dog. No heat is provided. These are mostly used on larger breeds to blast the water off the dog as it comes out of the bath. Some use it instead of towel drying. It may be used in combination with a hot air dryer as a finishing tool. The cost of these units is usually determined by their size and method of heat production. Dryers that use wire heating coils usually cost less than those of heating rod construction, although this in itself is no indication of the overall performance of either unit. I have still in use, as of this writing, a cage dryer of wire heating coil construction that is 21 years old. It has given me good reliable service for that many years, even though the manufacturer is no longer in business.

This simple unit contains a double squirrel cage blower, wire heating coils, and an off-on switch. The housing is of formed sheet steel with an expanded lath screen to protect the air intake. Simple and serviceable.

Many more sophisticated types of dryers are available today to meet the desires and requirements of professionals. A drying cabinet that can be divided to accept two smaller breeds combines dryer and caging in one unit.

The warm air is circulated through the unit with the dogs enclosed. Clear plastic doors allow the dogs to see and be seen as the process dries them.

Nail cutting tools

These are available in three styles, each with an advantage and disadvantage.

The most widely used is known as a guillotine trimmer. It is constructed so that the nail may be inserted in a opening in one of the shearing blades, encircling it so as to hold it as the other blade cuts through.

The proper way to use this device is to hold the immovable lever against the palm with the movable lever under the fingers. A squeezing action produces the power required to cut the nail.

Guillotine-type nail tools cannot be used on dewclaws that have grown circular or corkscrew shaped. These odd-shaped nails, usually found on Oriental breeds, can be trimmed with an alternate tool.

Pet nail scissors are, as the name implies, a side-cutting scissor-type tool. They have round loops for the insertion of thumb and finger and long leverage-gaining arms connecting to grooved-out cutting blades.

Because of their side-cutting action, they can engage and cut circular and corkscrew-shaped nails. Since only the thumb and finger are used to operate the tool, it may be necessary to use the free hand for added pressure in order to cut through some heavy nails. Bathing the dog prior to cutting can help soften nails to some degree.

Plier-type nail cutters operate similar to nail scissors. They are side-cutting tools that have the advantage of the guillotine cutter's powerful grip. The handles of the tool are long enough to grip in the hand, plier fashion. Some are affixed with a movable depth gauge that is supposed to prevent too deep a cut. This, however, depends upon how close the quick is to the portion being cut. In any case, multiple cuts with or without the depth gauge in place can still draw blood. The depth still must be visually judged, since the gauge simply gives a preset increment but doesn't stop excessive cutting.

Motor-driven nail grinders will create a tight compact-looking foot by rounding over the ends of the nail. A sanding disk, drum, or small grindstone removes the excess nail by abrasion. Extreme care must be taken due to the speed at which these units operate. An off-on technique using a light touch is the best way to keep friction from overheating the nail and causing pain.

A combination of nail cutting and grinding may be employed for a safer approach. The nail is cut back to the proper length with the usual nail cutting tool and then the sharp edges smoothed with either electric or manual equipment.

Many dogs object to the vibration, and are sensitive to the heat created by these tools. It would be wise not to use these on delicate breeds and small breed puppies. If a smooth rounded nail is a must, a manual dog nail file, which has a groove for the nail to track in, is a good alternative.

If neither method is used, after a few short walks, freshly cut nails will round over and be blunt enough for the client's acceptance. Be prepared to spend more time on the nail cutting procedure with either of these methods due to the dog's reaction and the care involved. An additional service charge is warranted.

Caution: High speed nail grinding equipment will throw off filings, sand, and, if defective, pieces of grindstone. Protect your eyes and lungs from flying debris by wearing a protective eye and face shield.

Additionally, to avoid injury, be careful not to catch your own or the dog's long hair in electric rotary equipment. A protective nail groomer shield that attaches to the unit and helps protect against eye, lung, and hair snag injury is available. Known by the name Vac-U-Shield®, it fastens to the nail grinder and your own vacuum without tools. It is the best method to eliminate toxic dust and protect the eyes as well!

Mat splitters, combs and rakes

These devices, used properly, can make the grooming session more bearable for both dog and groomer when the coat condition warrants the use of these tools. These tools also allow you to save areas of the dog's coat that would probably be sacrificed otherwise.

Grooming tables for stationary and portable use

A prerequisite for any grooming table you may choose to work with is that it be sturdy, with a sure gripping work surface. Most animals will sit or stand on any type of table that doesn't wobble or have a slippery surface. If the table wobbles or shakes as the dog is standing, there is a great probability that the pet will jump from the table for fear of falling off. All dogs should be discouraged from jumping. It is poor control to let them know you will allow it, and they can suffer severe injury if their feet slip out from under them on the floor. It therefore is imperative that the table be balanced up prior to placing the dog on it. Since most tile floors are not perfectly even, this must be done each time a table may be moved if required.

A nonslip ribbed rubber top is preferable on the table. It provides good footing for the dog and may be sanitized as required.

The most commonly used grooming table is the folding or portable type. This usually is constructed of folding tubular legs attached to a wooden top covered with ribbed rubber. It is a simple and serviceable unit that is easily transported in one's automobile and set up by unfolding the legs, and you are ready to groom.

This type of table is available in a variety of sizes from 18″ to 24″ wide and from 30″ to 48″ long. The size chosen is determined by the size dog the groomer intends to handle.

For example, it is wise to use a smaller table (18″× 24″) for Toy and Miniature breeds. The dog stays positioned closer to you than it would be if a 48″ table were used. There is less tendency for it to roam on a smaller table.

Larger tables are a worthwhile investment, of course, if most of the business is conducted on large breeds. A 48″ table will give more stability as well as a greater standing area for the dog.

Additionally, there are electrically and hydraulically operated tables to adjust the height at will at the touch of a pedal. The electric tables may also be had with an illuminated top, at the loss of the nonslip feature. An electric motor activates the raising and lowering of the unit. Hydraulic tables rely on either electric power or foot pumping power to elevate or lower them from about 29″ to 40″.

These tables are naturally stationary units and are quite sturdy, and for the most part are used in the groomer's shop. They are available either as a round-cornered rectangle or oval-top design. Some have equipment drawers mounted under them. Most will have tops that can be rotated the same as a beauty salon chair, which may cause the dog to jump off if done with the animal in place on the table.

All tables are available with or may be adapted for the traditional adjustable metal grooming arm, used with a sliding noose to control the movement of the dog on the table. These are fastened around the dog's neck.

I never could or would advocate the use of a grooming arm and noose due to the potential injury and trauma to the trachea, esophagus, and cervical spine.

The sudden lunge of a puppy or weak older animal can cause a fall, which may end up with the animal hanging by the neck. Injury and death have been the outcome of some such incidents. The grooming arm and noose create a false sense of security that can encourage leaving the dog unattended.

My own methods, those taught to my students, start with the training of the dog to accept the table as a safe secure place rather than restrain them on it. Acceptance comes quickly and the whole grooming job becomes easier and safer: no grooming arm in the way, no injury to worry about.

Cages and alternate methods of confinement

Today's groomer has a wide variety of equipment to choose from, and caging is no different.

The type and size of the units must be well thought out as to the type and size of the dogs they must accommodate.

Although some breeds may be the same in overall size, the breeds may differ sufficiently to warrant a stronger-than-usual cage for the size.

Select a cage with too narrow a gauge door wire and a strong-mouthed pet will demolish it if he has a mind to. Be aware that most pets are not caged other than when they are kenneled, or make the scheduled grooming trip. Many will object fiercely to being enclosed in a cage.

Weak bars or wires that are only spot-welded will easily snap under the pressure of an irate terrier, small as it may be.

There also exists the danger of animals injuring themselves as they try to push past the closed doors. A broken grill becomes a deadly instrument, ready to poke out an eye or tear the mouth of the determined animal.

Some dogs shouldn't be put into a cage, or crate as those that fold up are called, at all. Here is what else you can do.

Arrange your shop so that you provide at least a few stations with benching. This arrangement is the same as seen at some dog shows. The bench is walled on three sides and a snap bolt fastening method is provided on the rear end wall.

A choker collar may be secured to the dog for speed of removal and replacement on the snap bolt. The floor of the bench is provided large enough so that, when secure, the dog may sit or lie down without being able to overhang or step off the edge.

In this way the more hyper animals may be confined in safety, to await their turn at the grooming table or to rest afterward.

Another advantage of benching is that you will seldom be faced with a snarling pet who won't let you remove him, as may be the case when caged.

Wire grill floor grates are available for most size cages. These prove a sanitary arrangement for those offending clients who haven't walked their dogs prior to being brought to the groomer. These also serve well for those small pups and geriatric pets who just can't wait till they go home.

Naturally the smaller-footed dogs and pups will have to be provided with a place of solid footing such as a piece of carpeting, towel, or folded newspaper.

To catch the liquid or solid droppings, a pan either zinc- or epoxy-coated may be slipped under the grate in the cage. These are conveniently located in most cages that provide for removal without having to remove the dog first.

Kennel cages, walled on five sides with the door in front, are usually of the best construction. These are the type seen in pet shops for long-term housing of dogs. They are made of fiberglass and resins. Some are stainless steel as used by many vets. Others are fine-finished Formica-covered wood. These three types are by far the most expensive.

They are excellent for large strong dogs, and convenient to use and keep sanitary. They are not essential, however, particularly for a shop specializing in small breed grooming.

Miscellaneous equipment

Your fine assortment of tools should have a home of its own. I never cared for drawers since it is necessary to open them in order to obtain the tool required. Then you have to close the drawer. Then you open it again to replace the tool. Seems like a lot of lost motion and time.

A framed peg board, with a shelf or two as part of the unit, makes more sense to me. A narrow shelf can hold all your blades, and peg board hooks your scissors, combs, nail clippers, etc. A screw hook or two are ideal secure ways to hang up the clipper, and a ribbon dispenser may be also affixed to the rack. The most convenient space-saving device holds finished bows in a vertical arrangement, each segregated by type and color, with an automatic dispensing closure method to keep them clean and floating dust and hair out. Marketed under the name Caddypillar®, it will prove to be a worthwhile addition to any shop.

Clippin' Sling™

Although not used by the vast majority of today's groomers because they never received training on it, I have always found the use of a Clippin' Sling™ invaluable, and have always trained my students in its proper use.

This hammock-type tool is more than useful in controlling the dog (see the chapter on shaving the feet). It also places the dog in a comfortable position that is safe for canine and groomer.

It is super for puppies. Its cradling effect soothes and calms them to the point that some will nap in it while you work on them.

It is great for geriatrics or other animals with arthritis or injured legs that are difficult for both dog and groomer to keep supported off the table.

Hard-to-control, sensitive-footed dogs of all breeds, sizes and ages succumb to the sling. When it comes to nail clipping, the procedure can be done out of strike range of the animal. The job is done efficiently and, most important, safely.

Other areas can also be clipped, such as the face and rear areas on dogs that just won't hold still on the table. Scissor trimming sensitive legs becomes a snap when they are just hanging in midair, suspended by the Clippin' Sling™. Slings, incidentally, are available in a variety of sizes to suit the requirement.

Although I have included them with miscellaneous equipment, I consider them a major tool I wouldn't be without. Once you use one, I am sure you will feel the same way.

Other tools may include Phillips and straight-blade screwdrivers and pliers for clipper maintenance. A scissor press or plier will let you adjust your scissor tension yourself when required. Clipboards to hold your working client cards make the job much easier. Keep one in your bathing station to identify each dog's bath requirements and check it off when done. It will save double work or missed services.

Don't forget to use an inexpensive scissor to cut your ribbon for bows. Using your fine groomer shears for this will ruin the set for fine hair trimming.

Grooming supplies required

The initial cash outlay for supplies can be minimal, and still give you all you need to start your operation satisfactorily.

Large quantity purchases will allow you to save some, but I would not encourage the new shop owner to tie up his capital in supplies until his business warranted it.

You will need the following items listed for the uses specified.

Shampoo

A variety exists in so great a number that you can be easily confused and misled by the labels. Just remember that no shampoo concentrate dilutes the same all over the country due to different water conditions. Also, some manufacturers tend to exaggerate: "One gallon of concentrate makes fifty gallons of shampoo," etc. No way!

Klip-Klot® styptic dispenser

This new, as of this writing, blood-stopping device lightens the chore of nail clipping. An internal mechanism automatically advances a steady supply of powdered blood-clotting material in an easily held container.

It is designed to apply the proper amount by simply inserting the dog's nail into the opening. When the nail is withdrawn, any excess is squeegeed off back into the dispenser, preventing accidental spillage and staining of the feet.

The automatic closure of the dispenser applicator orifice helps keep moisture out, to prevent hardening of the contents, and keeps the powdered product clean and sanitary. It prevents waste, which saves money too.

It is a welcome replacement for the old bottle cap, and similar crude styptic application methods.

Conditioner rinse and creme formulas

This concentrated liquid is applied diluted after the regular shampoo and is designed to make the coat more manageable by preventing static electric tangling, so that brushing and combing is easier to do. It is optional for use on short-haired pets, almost a must on longhairs.

Flea and tick dip concentrate

I prefer the biological organic dips for obvious reasons. One gallon of concentrate makes over 100 gallons of diluted, ready-to-use flea and tick dip. In that ration, it is cheap enough to use fresh each time, instead of recycling it as some would advocate.

By making a fresh batch for use each time, you can also be considerate and use warm water, for the comfort of the animal.

Hot oil treatments

Various products are on the market. Some suggest a special, their own, pre-treatment shampoo prior to application of their oil emulsion. All have some measure of value and add plus business to the grooming service fee.

Other supplies

You will require an assortment of other miscellaneous supplies to fully equip your grooming operation. A check list will include:

- Tissue and paper towels for cleanup.
- Disinfectant for cage and table, floor and tub cleaning and sanitizing.
- Cotton balls for ear cleaning.
- Alcohol for ear cleaning and foot swabbing.
- Ear powder for ear plucking.
- Conditioner coat spray.
- Cologne.
- Clipper lubricant spray.
- Terry cloth bath towels.
- Nail polish assortment.
- Nail polish remover.

- Petroleum jelly to cover sores prior to bath and dipping.

- Mineral oil for eyes when dipping.

- Rubber bands.

- Ribbon bows.

- Barrettes.

- Scratch pads.

- Receipt books.

- Client record cards or 3″ × 5″ cards.

- And of course, an appointment book.

Questions???

A question is always an indication that a person has an interest in the subject. Since we want interested persons as our clients, it is to the groomer's advantage to be able to answer them intelligently.

Your immediate knowledgeable response will mark you as a professional, one who knows the business and can be relied upon to be the caretaker of the family's beloved pet.

Never avoid answering a question, and if you don't know the answer, say so, and advise the client that you will attempt to find the answer if they are willing to call back in a short while.

This can be a helpful learning process for you as well, for once learned, you will always have a ready answer. Your client will appreciate your honesty rather than giving them a fast, unrealistic reply.

Many times, the difference between securing a new client and not will depend upon how well you were able to answer questions!

Below you will surely find some of the most often asked of the myriad of questions that you will eventually experience for yourself.

It will be most beneficial if you study the questions as they are presented and prepare enlightening answers to each one. Having a ready answer will enable you to master the situation and secure your appointments quickly, without loss of precious time.

Fifteen questions clients most frequently ask

1. How much do you charge?

2. Do you tranquilize the dogs?

3. Can I stay with my pet and watch?

4. What does the grooming consist of?

5. Will my dog be kept in a cage?

6. Is my dog old enough to be groomed?

7. How long will my dog have to stay for grooming?

8. Do you flea and tick dip with the grooming?

9. Gigi went into heat last night. should I cancel the appointment?

10. Will my pet's hair grow back again?

11. Can she get a bath in the winter?

12. Do you feed the dogs while they are being groomed?

13. Can you cut the nails very short?

14. Can you groom her so she looks like a show dog?

15. How often will my pet need to be clipped?

Consultation

Within these pages you will find a form which if used will provide you with a free brief consultation on any topic in this book. Simply fill out the form and enclose it with a *business-sized, stamped, self-addressed envelope!*

If you desire an audio cassette response, which can be more detailed, enclose $10 with your request to cover costs.

Commencement

So, you have thoroughly read, absorbed and practiced all that has been written within these pages. You're now ready!

For what, you ask?

To give your best shot at professional canine styling — of course!

You are now ready to leave the ranks of the amateur.

If the first sentence above truly applies to you, you have crawled enough by now, and now you are ready to walk, and then run. Congratulations are due you.

AND YOU CAN DO IT!

Remember this: The secret to Making Big Money Grooming Small Dogs is to obtain and then retain your clients. And that's done by becoming skillful and proficient in your craft. And THAT'S done through practicing what you've been instructed to do in this book!

Simply follow through with what you have learned and have practiced. You will find that there are many pet owners that are willing to pay you handsomely for the service you will enjoy providing.

And when they experience your expertise, they will return again and again, like clockwork, on time as appointed.

And when you groom your first dog as a professional, and feel that first rush of success, drop me a line and let me know of your experience, with a copy of your business card for my student success file. Good luck and happy grooming.

◆ ◆ ◆

Cosmetic Styling

The following flaws can be disguised, and the animal made visually more appealing,
provided that the dog's coat is of good texture and fullness.
One that is dense, coarse & stands up easily is best.

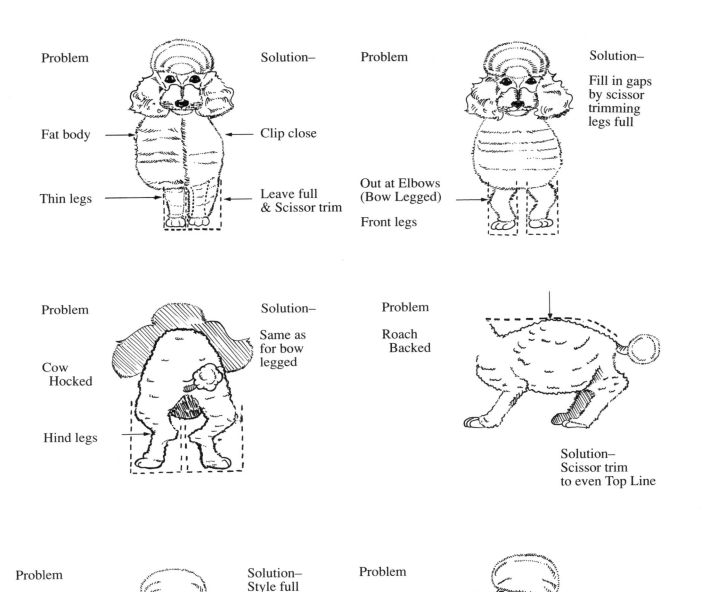

Problem

Fat body

Thin legs

Solution–

Clip close

Leave full
& Scissor trim

Problem

Out at Elbows
(Bow Legged)

Front legs

Solution–

Fill in gaps
by scissor
trimming
legs full

Problem

Cow
Hocked

Hind legs

Solution–

Same as
for bow
legged

Problem

Roach
Backed

Solution–
Scissor trim
to even Top Line

Problem

Undershot Jaw

Solution–
Style full
Mustache–
Trim to
smooth
line

Problem

Overshot Jaw

Solution–
Style
Mustache &
Goatee.
Trim to
cover
Short Jaw

If the dog has high set ears – Trim a large pom-pom
If the dog has low set ears – Trim a smaller pom-pom

Illustrated Glossary

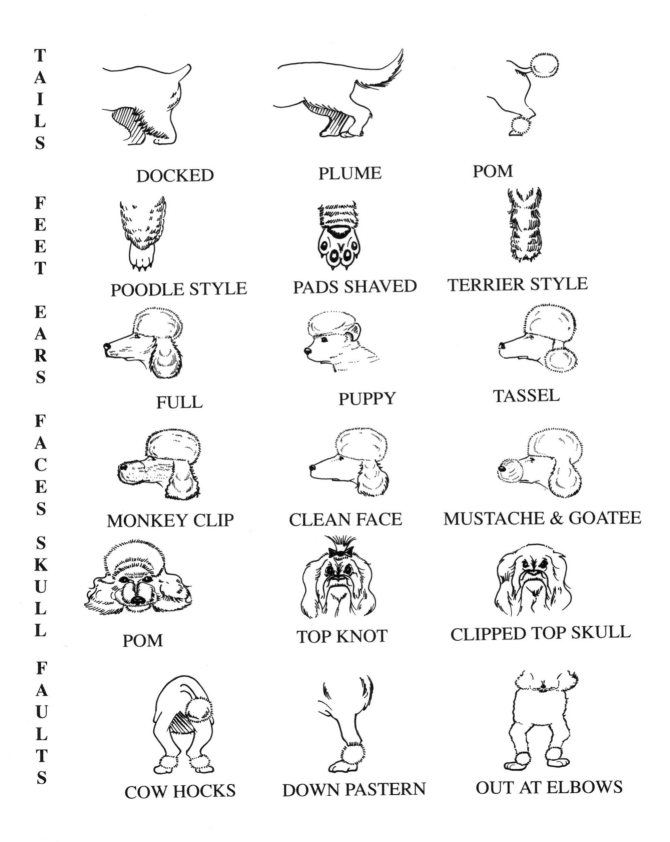

TAILS

DOCKED PLUME POM

FEET

POODLE STYLE PADS SHAVED TERRIER STYLE

EARS

FULL PUPPY TASSEL

FACES

MONKEY CLIP CLEAN FACE MUSTACHE & GOATEE

SKULL

POM TOP KNOT CLIPPED TOP SKULL

FAULTS

COW HOCKS DOWN PASTERN OUT AT ELBOWS

Index

Important Notes

CUT OUT ALONG DOTTED LINE — PHOTOCOPIES NOT ACCEPTED!

TO: Protective Specialties Development Group
      P.O. Box 39060
      Philadelphia PA 19136

FROM:

Today's date _____   Date book purchased _____

Name _____

Address _____

City _____   State _____   Zip _____

FREE BRIEF REPLY CONSULTATION FORM

Instructions

Use this side of paper only. Print or type your question on any topic in this book. We cannot respond to handwritten inquiries. Enclose a #10 (long) self-addressed stamped envelope for reply.

☐ I'm requesting an audio cassette taped reply **in detail.** Find my check or money
   order # _____ for $10.00 enclosed.

Form #FE94